MARCO  POLO

D1369097

VEN
ICE

GERMANY
LI
AUSTRIA
Innsbruck
SWITZER-
LAND
Bolzano
SLOVENIA
Milan
Venice
Genoa
CROATIA
ITALY
BOSNIA-
HERZEGOVINA
Gulf of
Genoa
Ancona
SAN
MARINO
Corsica
(F)
Adriatic
Sea
Rome

www.marco-polo.com

FREE!

THE TOURING APP

shows you the way...
including routes and offline maps!

GET MORE OUT OF YOUR MARCO POLO GUIDE

IT'S AS SIMPLE AS THIS

1 go.marco-polo.com/ven

2 download and discover

GO!

WORKS OFFLINE!

SYMBOLS

INSIDER TIP Insider-Tipp

★ Highlight

🔵🔵🔵🔵 Best of …

☼ Scenic view

Ⓡ Responsible travel: for
ecological or fair trade
aspects

(*) Telephone numbers
that are not toll-free

**PRICE CATEGORIES
HOTELS**

Expensive	over 190 euros
Moderate	115–190 euros
Budget	under 115 euros

Average prices for the cheapest double room. There can
be huge variations in price –
in both directions – depending on the season

**PRICE CATEGORIES
RESTAURANTS**

Expensive	over 45 euros
Moderate	20–45 euros
Budget	under 20 euros

Price for a threecourse meal,
typical for the particular
restaurant, without drinks

CONTENTS

DID YOU KNOW?
For bookworms and film buffs → p. 24
Time to chill → p. 32
Spotlights on sports → p. 44
Favourite eateries → p. 65
Local specialities → p. 68
More than a good night's sleep → p. 86
Public holidays → p. 105
Budgeting → p. 109
Fit in the city → p. 111
Weather → p. 112
Currency converter → p. 113

MAPS IN THE GUIDEBOOK
(120 A1) Page numbers and coordinates refer to the street atlas and the general map on p. 130/131
(0) Site/address located off the map

Coordinates are also given for places that are not marked on the street atlas

(🌐 A–B 2–3) refers to the removable pull-out map

(🌐 0) Site/address located of the map

INSIDE FRONT COVER:
The best highlights

INSIDE BACK COVER:
Plan of the *vaporetto* lines

The best MARCO POLO Insider Tips

Our top 15 Insider Tips

INSIDER TIP A look at everyday life

How did the 18th-century Venetians live? Daily life for the upper ten thousand with a stroll in the morning, a reception in the evening, rowing regatta and funeral celebrations is brought to life in the art displayed in the picture gallery of the *Museo Querini Stampalia* → p. 43

INSIDER TIP A head for heights

The most spectacular *spiral staircase* in Venice is on the Palazzo Contarini del Bovolo close to Campo Manin. Since its restoration, it has once again been open to visitors. A not-to-be-missed treat! → p. 38

INSIDER TIP At the youthful and inviting restaurant *Fantàsia*,

run by a charity organization, you can enjoy pizzas, pasta dishes or fish specialities while also helping those suffering from rare diseases or other handicaps → p. 69

INSIDER TIP Hidden treasures

A number of masterpieces by Tintoretto are hidden in the Gothic church of *Madonna dell'Orto*, which is slightly off the tourist track → p. 47

INSIDER TIP Dining on Murano

For creative cuisine and excellent wines, head to *Vecchia Pescheria* in a stylishly renovated old factory and its idyllic terrace → p. 68

INSIDER TIP A visit to the "dangerous deluded"

Many years ago, psychiatric patients were incarcerated on the tiny island of *San Servolo*. Today there is a museum that reminds us of the horrendous "treatment" methods of those days. Not for the faint-hearted! → p. 58

INSIDER TIP Aperitivo alla veneziana

Enjoy a glass of wine and some tasty snacks as the sun goes down – along with the bustle of the ever-popular *Osteria Bancogiro* on the fish market → p. 63

INSIDER TIP **Smart slip-ons**
Cooler than the coolest flip-flops: the non-slip, velvety-soft shoes worn by the gondolieri in *Piedàterre* → p. 75

INSIDER TIP **Spectacular views**
Instead of climbing up the bell tower of San Marco, where visitors end up treading on each other's toes, head for the *Campanile di San Giorgio Maggiore* on the island of the same name. It is close to St. Mark's Square, and the views are simply fabulous → p. 97

INSIDER TIP **A treat for the eyes and taste buds**
Individualists and gourmets have made themselves at home on the garden island of Mazzorbo in *Ostello Venissa*, just 30 minutes by boat from San Marco (photo below) → p. 88

INSIDER TIP **On the heels of maritime greatness**
Admire the collection of historic sailing vessels at the *Ships Pavilion* → p. 43

INSIDER TIP **Magic moments**
A sleepy square in San Polo is home to the 1000-year-old church of *San Giacomo dell'Orio*. Do not miss it – there is something truly special about the medieval ambience! → p. 49

INSIDER TIP **Explore the secret of the lagoon with children**
Travel through the silent, labyrinthine channels to the hidden areas of the lagoon by *bragozzi*, old-fashioned wooden barges → p. 102

INSIDER TIP **Wine from the vegetable island**
Stroll across the vegetable island of Sant'Erasmo and sample one of the wines grown here by an eccentric Frenchman – courtesy of the *Orto di Venezia* vineyard → p. 59

INSIDER TIP **Acqua alta equipment**
Brightly coloured rubber boots that add a touch of fun (and keep your feet dry) even in a flood can be purchased from *Acqua Marea* → p. 74

BEST OF ...

● *Basilica di San Marco – the treasure chest*
Admission to the grand, richly ornamented *St Mark's Basilica*, this orgy of gold, silver and precious stones, is free -- not only that, but from spring to autumn, guided tours to the gorgeous stone mosaics don't cost anything either → p. 33, 36

● *Feel a goose walk over your grave?*
The island of *San Michele* (photo) is home to the "celebs' cemetery" of the past: it is the final resting place of poets and thinkers, artists and industrialists. Visit their graves, and experience the atmosphere of this area (admission is free) – it's pure melancholy. And then hurry straight back to the hustle and bustle of St. Mark's Square! → p. 57

● *Partying under the stars*
Chatting with the locals while enjoying a glass of wine is easy, weather permitting, as many of the squares turn into proper open-air party venues where you don't have to buy drinks. Some of the most popular spots are the Campi *Santa Margherita* and *San Bartolomeo* → p. 80

● *Museum for your ears*
Listen to the hits of days long gone as Baroque music fills the air while you explore the exhibition of well-crafted flutes, violas, violins and lutes in the church of *San Maurizio* in the heart of San Marco → p. 36

● *Superlative painting*
What is supposedly the largest Baroque ceiling painting in the world is hidden behind the modest brick façade of *San Pantalon* church – a colossal work put together out of 40 individual canvas elements, freely accessible → p. 56

● *Relax under the trees*
The benches on the pretty *Campo San Giacomo dell'Orio* are perfect for a little rest. Just settle yourself down and watch the relaxed activity. It's better than the cinema – and it's free → p. 49

●●●● Dots in guidebook refer to "Best of..." tips

● *Travel the canals by gondola*

Tacky, but soooo nice! Instead of looking down your nose at all the tourists taking pictures of each other on the *gondolas*, why not try it yourself? Once you have glided through the silent canals, you'll understand its magic → p. 110

● *Sundowner or dinner on the Rialto*

Enjoy the specialities under the open sky: the *shore zone of the Canal Grande* between the fish market and Fabbriche Vecchie is the "in" district for fans of the open air → p. 76

● *Lively festivals*

The Venetians demonstrate their talent for celebrating at several smaller festivals worth attending throughout the year, including the *Asparagus Festival* in Cavallino, the *Fishermen's Festival of Malamocco* and the *Wine Festival on Sant'Erasmo* → p. 104, 105

● *Lace island*

Have you ever heard of a lacemaker? It used to be a very highly regarded profession, and Venetian lace was said to be the best on the world market. For several centuries, lacemaking provided the inhabitants of the island of *Burano* with a living. Find out all about it in the island's museum → p. 57

● *Bellini, Tizian, Tintoretto & Co.*

From momentous biblical scenes by the great masters of the Renaissance to the genre and landscape paintings of the Baroque and Rococo periods: nowhere else can art lovers find such a wealth from the quintessence of Venetian painting of this quality than in the *Galleria dell'Accademia* → p. 53

● *Lagune, mon amour*

The Venetian *Lagoon* is a unique eco system with plants and animals that are almost unique to this area. Travel the reed and marshland in tiny boats, and feel free to bombard the highly knowledgeable guides with questions! → p. 102

● *Long promenade on the water*

A stroll down the 1.2 km/0.75 mi *Zattere* quay in Dorsoduro with views of the Giudecca Canal will delight your heart. Enjoy the pure Venice feeling! (photo) → p. 52

ONLY IN

BEST OF ...

AND IF IT RAINS?
Activities to brighten your day

● *Discover the Doge's palace*
For almost 1000 years, 120 doges determined the fate of the Sea Republic from this gigantic complex of buildings. It is no wonder that the halls are so elaborately decorated (photo) → p. 38

● *Make your own mask*
They are one of the features of the Carnival in Venice: the artistic masks the costumed people wear. At *Ca' Macana*, you can not only buy one of these works of art but also spend a couple of hours learning how to make one → p. 74

● *The maritime heritage of the Republic of St. Mark*
A colourful collection of historic watercraft at the *Padiglione delle Navi* near the Ponte dell'Arsenale over the Rio della Tana brings to mind the glorious times of life at sea. An exciting exhibition that is also idea for children! → p. 43

● *Place your bets!*
If it rains, you can spend days in the noble atmosphere of Richard Wagner's final home playing roulette, blackjack or poker. The *Casino* is located in a magnificent Renaissance palace → p. 80

● *Art of the 20th century*
Modern art is a welcome change in a city that can look back over 500 years of painting. You will find works by all of the great masters of 20th century art in the *Collezione Peggy Guggenheim* → p. 53

● *Plush elegance*
At the Oriental Bar of the *Metropole* hotel, you will feel exactly as if you were on the legendary Orient Express that used to run between Venice and Istanbul. No stress, no worries, but sandwiches and excellent cakes and pastries → p. 84

RAIN

RELAX AND CHILL OUT
Take it easy and spoil yourself

● *Relax with music*

Monteverdi, Vivaldi, Albinoni: the ensemble *Interpreti Veneziani* offers a fine opportunity to hear works by the great masters of Renaissance and Baroque music. They give more than 200 concerts a year in the former San Vidal Church → **p. 80**

● *VIP-style chilling*

Venice has always been "in" with the international jet set. At the *B-Bar* in the luxury hotel The Bauer's, you'll be able to spot international stars passing by as you sip a mojito → **p. 78**

● *Take a dip at the Lido*

A day (or at least half a day) on the sandy beach at the *Lido* makes a welcome change from exploring the labyrinthine old city. You will be able to get your breath back relaxing in a deck chair or swimming in the Adriatic Sea (photo) → **p. 102**

● *Take a break in a green oasis*

Need to recover from sightseeing? A perfect place to do this is under the cypress trees in the *garden of the church of San Francesco della Vigna*. It is one of the green oases that the Venetians are now starting to rediscover → **p. 18**

● *A drink against a fabulous backdrop*

The terraces of waterside restaurants such as *Linea d'Ombra* are perfect for a spritzer or spumante before dining. Come between 6 and 7pm before the kitchen is open, and say you'd just like something to drink → **p. 67**

● *Massage in the garden*

Francesca Bortolotto Possati has brought four abandoned gardens on Giudecca back to life. At the *Palladio Hotel & Spa*, you can stroll through the landscape – and even enjoy a massage in the midst of the floral wonders. And there's a wonderful spa for those who wish to relax away from the hustle and bustle → **p. 86**

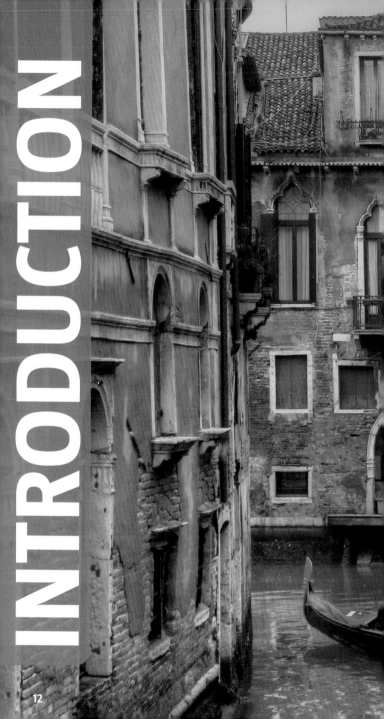

INTRODUCTION

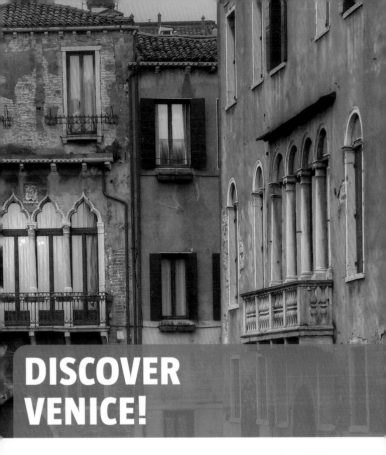

DISCOVER VENICE!

Venice is almost too much to take in at once. The city has 1000 facets, hidden corners, secret alleys. And whenever you think you've finally seen Venice as she truly is, the picture slips away from you again ... But just stay calm. After all, you don't have to understand the city from the very first day. And the more often you come, the more pictures you will see. There's the *postcard Venice*, rigid and lifeless, with stone bridges and palaces. Then there's *Disneyland Venice*, full of kitsch and cheap souvenir tat. And then there's the dream image that rises up out of the dirty water of the Canal Grande as you float by in a gondola, enraptured by the amazing façades of the *palazzi on the water*: fabulous and yet morbid. Precious frescoes and crumbling plaster. Testimonies to bygone power. The mind's eye sees the doge with his army of servants, the rustling gowns of the over-dressed Rococo ladies, and Giacomo Casanova himself lounging on a terrace.

In contrast, there's *everyday life* in the form of a cursing labourer balancing hand mixers and microwaves from a freight barge on his handcart to take to one of the few shops selling household goods. Children laughing in a school playground, dogs strolling along the Lido beach, old ladies shopping at the market near the Rialto bridge.

Life here is never boring. *Just relax and let life happen*, wander around the maze of alleys and lanes – little is more enjoyable–. There's always something new to discover. And not always art treasures! Of course, Venice has plenty of those, but by the same token it's not an open-air museum, but a living, lively city where people work and relax, love and argue.

It's easy to forget how tiring everyday life is, how many inconveniences the people who live here have to deal with. Being jostled every morning and evening, on the way to and home from work, by the vast numbers of day trippers in a *vaporetto*, or battling your way *up and down bridges through the flow of visitors* with a pram to the only remaining baker in the district. It's not all la dolce vita.

The amazing façades of the palazzi on the water

And bakers are becoming increasingly few and far between. As are butches and other independent shops who stock the everyday basics. You can earn more with souvenirs than with yoghurt and tinned tomatoes, which is why the number of "ordinary" shops has more than halved over the past 30 years.

Today's Venetians now do the big family shopping in the vast supermarkets on the mainland at the weekend. If indeed they even have a family: *Venice is ageing*, and children are scarce. Italy has one of the lowest birth rates in the world, and more so

Carnival is not the only festival celebrated on the streets of Venice: Festa del Redentore in July

in Venice than almost anywhere else. The demographic pyramid has been turned upside down, and today there are almost five times as many 60-year-olds in Venetians than there are under 20. Why? The costs for food and consumer goods of all kinds are higher in Venice than anywhere else, *everyday life is more difficult* and

> **Just relax and let life happen, wander around the maze of alleys and lanes – little is more enjoyable**

local taxes are hefty. But the main reasons young families are leaving is because real estate prices have soared as the result of mass tourism. Wealthy foreigners will buy an apartment in Venice regardless of what it costs, leaving locals with no chance of affordable living.

In the 1950s, the population of Venice was 175,000; today there are only 55,000, and every year a few hundred more move away. Usually only a few kilometres to *terraferma*, where everything is easier and more modern. For centuries, this fertile land was the domain of the *Venetian Maritime Republic*; it greatest expansion to the mainland was in the middle of the 15th century, when it assimilated towns and cities such as Treviso, Padua, Vicenza and Verona. But then the Ottomans conquered Constantinople, and from the 16th century were engaged in a bitter war with the Venetians for the Mediterranean trade centres. The beginning of the end of the powerful Serenissima.

Today, Venice is also a centre for science and research. And, of course, it also has a university – students from all over the world are drawn here in particular for its *architecture faculty*, who bring with them creativity and esprit. As a result, a lively and bubbly local and cabaret scene has developed in the quarters Dorsoduro and Cannaregio in particular that hardly any visitors know about. Thanks to the university, there are also a number of *student pubs with sensible prices*, as well as lounges and clubs for chilling and relaxing – to say nothing of the venerable coffee houses, eyewateringly priced exclusive restaurants and *original trattoria*.

This city on water is a miracle of humanity. Who on earth first had the crazy idea of building a town in the middle of a swamp? Venice was born out of need; its founding was an act of desperation:

Where else could the people go to escape persecution by the Huns and Lombards who, from the year 500, descended on the fertile mainland like locusts, stealing and pillaging? They fled to the marshes, to the malaria-infested no-man's-land that, over the centuries, became a 2.9 mi² artificially created urban area. It took millions of wooden posts and *over 400 bridges*. In the Middle Ages, Venice was divided into six districts, the *sestieri*.

The best known of them is San Marco, with the wonderful St. Mark's Square. The least touristy ones are Castello, the former working-class district, and Santa Croce. San Polo is the smallest one geographically, but has the second-biggest square, Campo San Polo. The two islands of Giudecca and San Giorgio Maggiore also belong to Dorsoduro and San Marco. Cannaregio is home to the former *Jewish ghetto*. Decreed by the Venetian doge as the first in the world 500 years ago, sadly it soon found many imitators. Venice generally set a number of standards, both good and bad. As a free maritime republic, the city traded with areas that were, at that time, unimaginably distant, and was indeed a *cultural melting-pot*. The upper classes were accordingly well-educated and cosmopolitan. And rich. Unbelievably rich! Spices, coffee and cocoa came to Europe via Venice. So it follows that the *very first coffee house* of the western hemisphere also opened in Venice. That was in 1647, under the arcades of St. Mark's Square.

A lively and bubbly local and cabaret scene

Since then, the Venetians have been *masters of the arrangiarsi*, the art of getting along. They've got trade in their blood – and a keen sense for commerce. That was already so in 1204 when, under the leadership of the completely blind doge Enrico Dandolo, they unceremoniously diverted the fourth crusade to Constantinople to plunder the treasures of their fellow Christians. And it applied even more so over the following centuries, when the doges brutally represented the Republic's interests both internally and externally, and Venice was simply raking in the money as the *most important trading power in the eastern Mediterranean*. Skilled communicators, because also pretty brazen and stuck-up, the Venetians treated its competing Italian neighbours impertinently and arrogantly. The Duchy of Milan, in particular, was a tedious antagonist that Venice squabbled with for centuries.

However, the tide has turned in recent decades. Formally, Venice is still the *capital of the Region of Veneto*, corporate but Veneto's heart now beats in the boom towns on the mainland. International groups were born here, such as Benetton, the gigantic clothing company, as well as Diesel and Stefanel, and the energy company ENI in the Venetian suburb of Marghera. There have long been plans to link this conurbation with some 2.5 million inhabitants and a workforce of more than 1 million people in a dynamic metropolis and create a modern major harbour of significance to the entire Mediterranean at Chioggia. But, as is so often the case in Italy, there's a lot of talking, discussion and arguing – and then everything is put on the back burner for now.

There is another, rather embarrassing story involving MOSE (Modulo Sperimentale Elettromeccanico), the proposed *flood protection project*. Allegedly a once-in-a-century undertaking, but above all a licence to print money for corrupt managers and politicians. Over a million euros have been misappropriated so far, and the head of the Venetian water authority ended up in jail along with the then

> **The very first coffee house in the western hemisphere**

mayor. The gentlemen had their sights on their bank accounts rather than on the lagoon. The Venetians call it *una vergogna*, a disgrace; they never really warmed to the idea of this vast flood protection system. Many of them simply don't like the thought of interfering with nature in such a radical way, and feel that wellies are a much easier solution.

The gondola pier at San Marco is only this empty during the (very) early morning hours

Around 30 million tourists visit Venice every year, and that number is constantly increasing. It's not doing the lagoon's fragile ecosystem any good – but how to handle this challenge? *Limit* the number allowed in? Charge an entry fee? Ask the Venetians, and you'll get so many different opinions that you'll be utterly confused yourself. One thing is certain, though: Venice is far from dead, *Venice is very much alive*. So don't wait any longer, but throw yourself into its fabulous chaos!

WHAT'S HOT

1 Creative hotbed

Hotspot for young creatives Hidden gems in Dorsoduro display works by young artists. For instance *PieM.Art (Calle Crosera 3751a)*, which sells photos and posters of Venice. With its high-quality changing exhibitions, the gallery of contemporary art *Marignana Arte (Rio Terà Catecumeni 141 | www.marignanaarte.it)* is more for looking at than shopping. Art and cold drinks are served in the gallery café, *Imagina Café (Campo Santa Margherita 3126 | www.imaginacafe.it)*.

Green Venice

2

Not only water The Venetians have started to rediscover the treasures of their green gardens – and are making them accessible to tourists. You can visit the absolutely non-touristy *Parco Savorgnàn (Canale di Cannaregio)* with its old laurel trees, and the mature trees in the small *Parco Villa Groggia (Fondamenta dei Reformati)* on your own. ● The garden of *San Franceso della Vigna church (Campo San Franceso della Vigna)* is a green oasis and a wonderful place to relax in the shade of its cypresses after a busy day sightseeing.

3 Keeping with the times

Contemporary art There are many interesting galleries in San Marco: *La Galleria Van der Koelen (Calle Calegheri 2566)*, whose owners focus on bringing international avant-garde art into the lagoon; *Galleria Traghetto (Campo Santa Maria del Giglio 2543)*, which specializes in niche styles; *Jarach Gallery (Campo San Fantin 1997)*, which is the best address for contemporary photography; and *Caterina Tognon Arte Contemporanea (Calle del Dose 2746 | photo)*, which hosts solo exhibitions by established as well as up-and-coming artists.

Stand-up rowing

Back to the roots Rowing standing up is an age-old technique from the times of the Serenissima. Known as *voga alla veneziana* in Italian, it had been forgotten for centuries – which is hardly surprising, as it's not a particularly efficient way of getting around. But it is an ancient tradition – and one that is loved by the Venetians of today. People row in twos or fours on a stand-up board, or paddleboard, which is a very flat boat with very little water resistance. But never make the mistake of telling a Venetian how similar they are to a gondola, or you'll end up having such a long discussion that you won't have time to row … Would you like to try this? Then come along to the *L'Altra Venezia (www. laltravenezia.it)* sports club and have a go!

4

Into the wild

Outdoor nights Hello – who's that lying there in the grass? Don't be surprised if you stumble over any Venetians camping in the outdoors if you visit any of the smaller lagoon islands. Just packing up a tent and spending a night outdoors is something that is hugely popular with the younger locals. Of course, the law enforcers and conservationists don't like it, but no sooner are the tents up than they disappear again. And although you're under no obligation to do the same, spending a night away from the city bustle and just listening to the frogs croaking as you nod off rather than people arguing under your window is an experience – and furthermore one that isn't expensive, for instance on the island Sant'Erasmo: *Il Lato Azzurro (www. latoazzurro.it)*

5

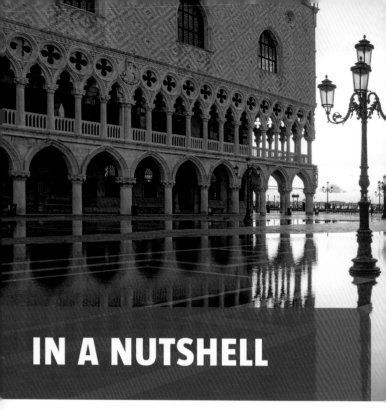

IN A NUTSHELL

DO YOU SPEAK VENEXIANO?

Between themselves, the Venetians speak the dialect they have used since time immemorial as a sign of their self-esteem. In some aspects, it is similar to Spanish and follows its own rules not only in terms of pronunciation but also in spelling and grammar. The people who live on the lagoon love to contract long (place) names. For example, San Zanipolo is an abbreviated form of the famous church of Santi Giovanni e Paolo, and San Zan Degola (John the Beheaded) is San Giovanni Decollato. Other characteristics: many consonants are voiced; a typical case is *amico* that turns into the Spanish-sounding *amigo*. In Venetian a sharp "s" often takes the place of the Italian

ch and *sh* sounds – *cento* is pronounced *sento*. And, "z" often becomes an "x". A classic example is one you will notice on advertisements for many trattorias: *cucina venexiana*.

HOW THE WELLINGTON, OR RUBBER, BOOT CAME TO VENICE

Venice is up to its neck in water. The waters of the Adriatic flood St. Mark's Square and large areas of the centre. Wading through knee-high water in wellies is something tourists find rather amusing, but for the Venetians it's a constantly recurring nightmare. The problem has existed for as long as Venice has, and it's gotten worse in the past 50 years. There are many reasons for

Wet feet and unaffordable apartments, tender vegetables and a lioness with wings: aspects of a very special city

this, but some of them are of their own making: man has interfered with the delicate ecosystem by digging out access channels for oil tankers on the way to Marghera, and cheerfully pumped out groundwater to fill the needs of industry on the mainland. So what to do? The mammoth MOSE (Modulo Sperimentale Elettromeccanico) project began in 2003. It comprises 78 steel barriers that are to be rooted at the three entrances to the lagoon and lift up automatically when there is a risk of flooding to seal off

Venice. Environmental organisations are sceptical. The floods of the Adriatic wash harmful substances out of the lagoon; without this exchange of water, the lagoon would be destroyed by its own dirt. Lauded by Italian politicians as a masterpiece of Italian engineering skills, MOSE itself is now at risk of going under: in a swamp of corruption. More than 30 contractors, administration managers and politicians, including Giorgio Orsoni, the former mayor of Venice, have been arrested for misappropriating funds. A healthy proportion of the 5.5 million euros that the lock system is to cost has been fed into foreign countries through accounts in San Marino. The Venetians are appalled. And will continue to reach for their wellies when necessary. You'll find a few impressive photos of "Venice flooded" e.g. at *short.travel/ven12* and *short.travel/ven11*.

THE DARK SIDE OF THE FORCE

Were these men really to be envied? As a doge, they took on the highest office the most powerful city state on earth had to offer and were then not allowed to leave the Republic without permission. They were neither allowed to choose their advisors themselves nor receive emissaries in private. Accepting gifts was just as forbidden as going to a café or theatre let alone abdicating of their own accord. They were not even allowed to write letters to their wives without it passing through the censor's hands. And, after the 11th century, they didn't even have any real power. Starting in 697, they reigned high-handedly and autonomously as medieval sovereigns. They negotiated with emperors and popes, decided on war or peace independently and even named their own successor. However, in 1032, a doge fell victim to his own lust for power and his attempts to institute a hereditary character for the office. In a flash, both he and his son were assassinated and the authority of his successors radically restricted. Degraded to simple executive officers, they were placed under the surveillance of the infamous Council of the Ten, a kind of medieval state security service. In later years this led to hardly any halfway capable person being prepared to accept what had once been such a prestigious office.

OLD BAGS AND YOUNG VEGETABLES

The fruit and vegetable market on the Rialto Bridge is in a central location right at the heart of the city's tourist area – and yet it is an extremely Venetian place. Early in the morning you'll hear scraps of dialect as Signora Maria inspects the aubergines on offer from Vincenzo and asks him when he's finally going to get the tender young artichokes from Sant'Erasmo Island back in again. Yes, that's right. Most of the vegetables are actually grown in the lagoon, rather than being carted in from far away. Sant'Erasmo is Venice's kitchen garden, where the people make a living from agriculture rather than tourism. Which means they tend vegetable beds rather than hotel beds. The question is how much longer will they be doing this. The islanders are becoming fewer and getting older. Vincenzo is in his early sixties, and is considered a spring chicken. His sons moved onto the mainland years ago. Who will still be around in 20 years' time to grow the typical purple artichokes is anyone's guess. So perhaps you'd better head to Sant'Erasmo island sooner rather than later.

BLACK, SLENDER AND CHIC

They are a little over 10 m/almost 33 ft long and almost 1.5 m/about 5 ft wide, weigh 350 kg/770 lbs empty, and consist of a total of 280 individual elements including the walnut oarlock *(forcola)* and seven-pronged iron prow *(ferro)* that weighs 20 kg/44 lbs. It is estimated that around 10,000 gondolas were in operation on Venice's canals in the 16th century. Today, only about 400 gondolieri are still active. However, there can be no talk about an end coming to the gondola business. Thanks to the trade being passed on within the family, there is no difficulty in finding recruits and, in spite of five months of slow business in the off season, also no financial problems. The order books of the *squeri* – the gondola shipyards – the most photogenic of which can be visited on Campo San Trovaso not far from the Zattere –, are full for years to come. A newly built boat, painted in traditional black, will set the new owner back about 13,000 £/ 17,000 US$.

and squares become peopled by all the characters from the commedia dell'arte. For centuries, this masquerading made it possible for Venetians to escape the watchful eye of the state for a short time at least. The occupier Napoleon, however, was suspicious and thought that conspiracy could flourish behind the masks and completely forbid the masquerade.

These spicy little things hail from Venice's vegetable island: *peperoncini* from Sant'Erasmo

COMPETITION OF THE MASKS

The city on the lagoon turns into a fairy-tale land in the last one and a half weeks before Lent when tens of thousands of people wander through Venice in their imaginative robes and its streets

It was not reintroduced until 1979.

Since then, hoteliers, restaurant owners and sponsors rub their hands in glee when hosts of people from all over the world, craving fun and masquerading, make their way to the city every year in what used to be the off-season in winter to pose, promenade around the city and, if their finances allow it, throw private parties in rented palaces. And, although very few locals mingle with the masses, and the number of spectators and paparazzi probably far exceed those in disguise, (and although plain Mickey Mouse, King Kong and Maya the Bee masks can be seen among the classical costumes), everybody agrees that being there and the unique atmosphere still compensate for the trip and the often drastically increased room rates.

THE FIRST WORLD TRAVELLER

Of course, he deserves special mention in a guidebook that is named after him seeing that Marco Polo, who was born in Venice in 1254 and died there 70 years later, is still considered the epitome of the (world) traveller driven by a yearning to see distant places and a thirst for knowledge. The merchant's son was only an adolescent when he set out across the Adriatic on his way to Asia; he spent many years in China and only returned by sea to the lagoon 24 years later. In Genoese custody, he later dictated his travel report *Il Milione* to a fellow prisoner; it became a bestseller in the Middle Ages and played a decisive role in shaping the Europeans' geographical notion of Asia. The Polo family's house was located not far from Rialto Bridge where the Teatro Malibran stands today.

DISNEYLAND SAYS HELLO

The number of shops selling souvenirs or – let's be honest here – cheap tat at exorbitant prices has exploded in recent years. By contrast, bakers, butchers and grocers have disappeared from the alleys, and the Venetians are obliged to do their big weekly shop at the supermarkets on the mainland. It's a fact: 10 million tourists are more lucrative than just under 100,000 locals. Absurd? No; it's the sad truth, and one that the Association of Young Venetians is fighting. It is insisting that the municipal administration adopt countermeasures. Young couples are unable to afford the high property prices, and are being driven out of their own city, they complain. They don't want their home town to be a Disney-

FOR BOOKWORMS AND FILM BUFFS

Don't Look Now – Crime writers are especially inspired by the unique, melancholy atmosphere: Daphne du Maurier set her short story, which was sensitively filmed in 1973 by Nicholas Roeg, in Venice

Those Who Walk Away – Patricia Highsmith's thriller also takes place in the floating city

Commissario Brunetti – An essential companion for visitors to Venice; the Venetian-by-choice Donna Leon has written more than two dozen crime stories featuring the police commissioner – so far

Death in Venice – Unadulterated melancholy characterises Thomas Mann's legendary novella. Luchino Visconti's film (1971) is one of the all-time classics

Don Giovanni – Venice plays a picturesque main role in Joseph Losey's adaptation of Mozart's opera as well as in Federico Fellini's film Casanova (1976)

land, an artificial world with no real inhabitants. Because if one day there are no locals left, then the tourists will stop coming too.

A LION NAMED MARKUS

No, the Venetians were not the only people to take the lion as their heraldic animal. But nobody else gave the king of the beasts two wings and placed a book between its front paws. There are different explanations of why this strange hybrid creature should represent Saint Mark of all people. Today, the number (and number of different forms) of the stone big cat are bewildering. You will see the Lion of Saint Mark on façades, cornices and capitals, on chimneys, graves, flowerpots, paintings, and statues of him out in the open.

G ENTRIFICATION ALLA VENEZIANA

The waters around Venice's *centro storico* are sprinkled with little islands, many of which have a quite special history. Poveglia's former – and future! – uses are particularly interesting. This island in front of the Lido in the south of the lagoon may only measure 17.3 acres, but it was once a sanctuary for deposed doges and a quarantine station when epidemics raged. In the 20th century, however, the island along with its few desolate buildings, vineyards and fruit trees fell into a deep sleep. It was unexpectedly awakened from its slumber in 2014 when the Italian government decided to quickly privatize a number of prime pieces of real estate to help alleviate its major budget deficit. The jewel in the crown, so to speak, was to be the island of Poveglia – the last open patch of land in the lagoon city. But a group of strong-minded Venetians decided to put a spoke in the government's plans because they

A half mask is a must for Carnival

did not like the idea that another island would be transformed into a luxury resort by a well-heeled hotel chain. Under the motto *Poveglia per tutti* (Poveglia for all), they launched a Facebook campaign to encourage their fellow citizens to fork out 99 euros a piece to collectively buy the rights to the island for 99 years. The proclaimed goal was to "turn the island into a public park in which children can play and friends can have grill parties". After the decisive Internet auction, the responsible authorities did in fact decline the highest lease offer from a real estate speculator – a half million euros – as insufficient. Thus, for the time being, the island remains in the hands of the state, and who knows, maybe it really will be opened to the public.

SIGHTSEEING

WHERE TO START?
Once you arrive in Venice, head for the **Piazza San Marco (126 C3)** *(ᗰ J–K 7–8)* first of all – preferably on board one of the Line 1 or 2 *vaporetti* that travel along the Canal Grande from the railway station, coach and car parks on Piazzale Roma. The 4.1/4.2 and 5.1/5.2 lines are also a good way to become acquainted with Venice as they travel around the entire old town.

The best bird's eye panoramas are from the viewing galleries in the Campanile of San Marco or San Giorgio Maggiore.

Straight into the thick of things with a ride on a *vaporetto*, across the Canal Grande – there's no lovelier way to start your Venetian adventure.

The Canal Grande is the main traffic hub. It's where gondolas glide and motorboats manoeuvre around barges and passenger boats against the backdrop of horns and curses. Full braking and bold moves: the Canal Grande is the Venetians' motorway – and we all know how the Italians drive.

It's a spectacle that begins at the station or the Piazzale Roma and takes you past the fabulous façades of palaces and churches as if you were on a personalised sightseeing tour. But you'll still have to walk and it would be a shame if you didn't. Because Venice's alleys are a

Photo: Canal Grande and the Santa Maria della Salute Church

A maze of stone as one complete work of art: magnificent palazzi, world-famous bridges and museums and atmospheric squares

maze made of stone, and you'll always find the best parts when you find you have taken the wrong way – again.

Venice is divided into six districts, the *sestieri*. At first glance, you might think that their labyrinths of streets all look the same. But each one of the six *sestieri* has its own, absolutely individual flair, although one thing applies to them all: it is not always possible to plan your route exactly. There is no reason why you shouldn't let chance guide you for a couple of hours. The only way to get to know

the hidden, tranquil sides of what is really Venice with its countless small attractions is by making – sometimes involuntary – detours and roundabout paths that will open up views of its cul-de-sacs and back courtyards. And, if you should get the feeling that you are well and truly lost, you will come across a yellow sign pointing to "Rialto", "San Marco" or the "Ferrovia" (railway station) on one of the next corners.

Even if one omits its churches overflowing with art treasures, Venice has several

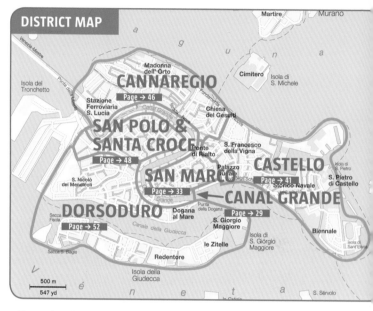

DISTRICT MAP

Murano
Martire
Venezia-Mestre
Isola del Tronchetto
CANNAREGIO
Page → 46
Madonna dell' Orto
Cimitero
Isola di S. Michele
Stazione Ferroviaria S. Lucia
Chiesa del Gesuiti
SAN POLO & SANTA CROCE
Page → 48
Ponte di Rialto
S. Francesco della Vigna
S. Nicolò del Mendicoli
SAN MARCO
Page → 33
Palazzo Ducale
CASTELLO
Page → 41
Isola di S. Pietro
S. Pietro di Castello
Storico Navale
CANAL GRANDE
DORSODURO
Page → 52
Dogana al Mare
Punta della Dogana
Page → 29
S. Giorgio Maggiore
Biennale
Isola di Sant'Elena
Sacca Fisola
Canale della Giudecca
Isola di S. Giorgio Maggiore
Sacca S. Biagio
le Zitelle
Redentore
Isola della Giudecca
S. Servolo

500 m
547 yd

The map shows the location of the most interesting districts. There is a detailed map of each district on which each of the sights described is numbered

dozen museums – ranging from world-famous temples of art such as the accademia, the Doge's Palace or the Collezione Peggy Guggenheim, to comparatively small collections of Murano glass, lace and Judaica, writings and objects of the Jewish culture and religion, that are well-worth seeing.

The city has mainly its former power to thank for this abundance. The doges themselves, with their desire for prestige and their mania for collecting, amassed paintings and other valuable objects from all parts of their maritime realm and employed the best architects, painters and craftsmen at home in the city on the lagoon. With their sense of style and generosity, the nobility and rich merchant families also played a major role in assembling the wealth of unique art treasures that we can feast our eyes on today.

The *scuole* are something typically Venetian. These are fraternities whose members perform charity work in the name of their patron saint to benefit less privileged sections of the community. Some of their most impressive assembly houses are of inestimable value and are now open to the public as museums.

The fact that the opening times and the days they are closed vary greatly and change frequently is rather impractical. And the conditions for reduced admission also vary a lot. In any case, it is always a good idea to ask if you can enter and have your passport or other means of identification with you.

Entrance fees for museums start at 5 euros (Museo Storico Navale) and go up to 10 or 12 euros (Scuola Grande di San Rocco and Accademia respectively). The "I Musei di Piazza San Marco" pass costs 19 euros and makes it possible to visit the four museums on Piazza San Marco. The "Museum Pass" for 24 euros includes all of the city's museums except the clock tower and the Palazzo Fortuny. EU citizens under the age of 18 have free entrance to the three state museums – Accademia, Galleria Franchetti and Museo d'Arte Orientale –, 18–25-year-olds are granted a reduction.

The Tourism Association's website *www.veneziaunica.it* gives the best overview on the internet (also in English and easy to navigate). All city museums are presented under *www.visitmuve.it* (also in English).

Fifteen of the most important churches in art history have joined forces to form the *Associazione Chiese di Venezia/Chorus* (tel. 04 12 75 04 62 | *www.chorusvenezia. org*). The Chorus Pass, a joint ticket for 12 euros (8 euros for students under 29, families 24 euros) makes it possible to visit these houses of worship and is valid for an unlimited period. Individual entrance to the important churches costs around 3 euros.

CANAL GRANDE

Most visitors to Venice gain their initial and lasting impressions of the beauty and uniqueness of this city on board a *vaporetto* on the Canal Grande.

Travelling along this winding waterway between the Dogana del Mar, the old customs house crowned with a golden globe, and the railway station or car park on Piazzale Roma (journey time from 15 to 40 minutes) is like moving past a

MARCO POLO HIGHLIGHTS

guard of honour made up of magnificent palaces and churches. As an exception, the most important architectural monuments along the route are listed here in their topographic order from north-west to south-east instead of alphabetically in order to make orientation less complicated.

PONTE DELLA COSTITUZIONE
(120 B6) (*ØJ C–D5*)

It's a real bone of contention, this modern bridge with the glass parapets and a herringbone design. Some people think it's as ugly as can be; others think it's great. Its creator and the municipality have even battled it out in court. What there is no denying is that this 94-m/308.4-ft pedestrian bridge, which was designed by Santiago Calatrava and has spanned the Canal Grande between Piazzale Roma and the station since 2008, is something completely different. *Stop: Piazzale Roma, Ferrovia*

FONDACO DEI TURCHI (121 F5) (*ØJ G4*)

The complex of buildings opposite the San Marcuola *vaporetto* stop was erected in the 13th century. 400 years later, Turkish merchants lived and carried out their business here leading to the name that is commonly used today. A rather insane total redevelopment in the 19th century robbed it of its Venetian-Byzantine character. Only the characteristic towers on the sides and the wide columned hall in between have been preserved. Today, the prominent building is the site of the Museum of Natural History (*Museo di Storia Naturale* | *June–Oct Tue–Sun 10am–6pm, Nov–May Tue–Fri 9am–5pm, Sat/Sun 10am–6pm* | *msn.visitmuve.it*) – great for families! The highlights include the aquarium and a dinosaur hall with a complete skeleton found in the South Sahara. *Stop: San Stae*

PALAZZO VENDRAMIN-CALERGI
(121 F4) (*ØJ G4*)

This imposing Renaissance palace built by Mauro Codussi and the Lombardo brothers around 1500 is firmly located in history as the place where Richard Wagner lived for a period before he died there on 13 February 1883. A commemorative plaque recalls that memorable day. Today, this is a gamblers' mecca; the city's casino (*www.casinovenezia.it*) with its night club are located behind the windows with their round arches. *Stop: San Marcuola*

SAN STAE (121 F5) (*ØJ G4*)

The main attraction of this 17th-century church is the beautiful Palladian-style façade added by the Swiss architect Domenico Rossi in 1709. There are several remarkable paintings from the early 18th century, including works by Giambattista Tiepolo, Giovanni Battista Piazzetta and Sebastiano Ricci, inside. *Campo San Stae 3013* | *Mon–Sat 2pm–5pm* | *stop: San Stae*

CA' PESARO (122 A5) (*ØJ H4*)

Even those who are not especially interested in the collections of oriental and modern art that are housed here should take a closer look at this massive Baroque complex with its marble façade that dominates the southern side of the Canal Grande, just two small canals away from the San Stae *vaporetto* stop. It is Baldassare Longhena's masterpiece and its construction took almost 60 years to complete. The interior is dominated by the forecourt and enormous vestibule. The splendid collection in the *Galleria d'Arte Moderna* of the Ca' Pesaro includes works by Max Klinger, Gustav Klimt, Wassily Kandinsky, Max Klee, Auguste Rodin, Marc Chagall and Giorgio De Chirico. Admirers of art from the far-east will find

The elegant curves of Calatrava's Ponte della Costituzione crossing over the Canal Grande

what they are looking for in the INSIDER TIP *Museo d'Arte Orientale* on the top floor with its collection of armour, textiles and artworks from China, Japan and Indonesia, as well as an important exhibition of Japanese paintings from the Edo period from the early 17th to mid-19th centuries. *Tue–Sun 10am–5pm, April–Oct until 6pm | capesaro.visitmuve. it | stop: San Stae*

CA' D'ORO/GALLERIA GIORGIO
FRANCHETTI (122 A–B5) (*ca H4–5*)

Nowhere else along the Canal Grande can you find a façade that is more delicate and precious than this one. The "Golden House" is the masterwork of the Venetian late-Gothic period at the transition to the Renaissance. Its painstakingly restored exterior, which was originally decorated with gold leaf and coloured marble, looks like Burano lace carved out of stone. INSIDER TIP *Baron Franchetti's art collection* is exhibited inside. It includes several masterpieces such as Andrea Mantegna's St Sebastian, Titian's Venus, Vittore Carpaccio's Annunciation and Death of the Blessed Virgin, as well

as paintings by Giovanni Bellini, Giorgione, Anthony van Dyck and many other artists. There is also an admirable collection of Flemish tapestries and Gothic and Renaissance furniture. *Tue–Sun 8.15am–7.15pm, Mon 8.15am–2pm | www.cadoro.org | stop: Ca' d'Oro*

PESCHERIA (122 B5) (*ca H5*)

The neo-Gothic building with its arcades was only constructed in 1907. However, a fish market has been held on this location since the 14th century and the neighbouring fruit and vegetable market ever since 1100. *Stop: Rialto or Ca' d'Oro and cross with the traghetto (gondola ferry)*

CA' FOSCARI (125 D–E3) (*ca F7*)

When you get to the *volta*, the last bend in the Canal Grande, look out for the entirely symmetrical façade of this late-Gothic palace. It was restored in 2008 by students of the university, which has its headquarters here. The palazzo used to belong to the family of the doge Francesco Foscari. In the 19th century it was used as a hospital, and later as a military barracks by the Austrian occupying forces. After that it was rather run-down, but thankfully some students like to roll their sleeves up and get on with things. And looking as it does today, it is once again a shining light on the Canal Grande. *Stop: Ca' Rezzonico, San Tomà*

PALAZZO GRASSI (125 E3) (*∅ F8*)

That's a fabulous building, sliding by on the other side of the water. The changing exhibitions have been the subject of much talk for several years now. Its French patron François Pinault spares no costs when it comes to making Venice a hotspot of contemporary art. *Wed–Sun 10am–7pm | Combined ticket with Punta della Dogana | www.palazzograssi.it | stop: San Samuele*

CA' REZZONICO/MUSEO DEL SETTECENTO VENEZIANO (125 D–E4) (*∅ F8*)

Even by Venetian standards, the massive palace built by Baldassare Longhena and Giorgio Massari is a special jewel of Renaissance architecture. For part of the 18th century, it was owned by Carlo Rezzonico who later wrote history as Pope Clemens XIII. Today, the building is home to the *Museo del Settecento Veneziano* and impressively documents the opulent lifestyle of the aristocracy in the late period of the Republic. The "Museum of the 18th Century" is spread over the three floors of the palazzo. Meticulously renovated, the priceless furniture and decorations, paintings and ceiling paintings on display provide an authentic impression of how the wealthy noble families lived during that high point in Venice's history. The carved furnishings, ceiling frescos and cabinet paintings with scenes of everyday life in Venice by Pietro Longhi are particularly outstanding. *Entrance: Fondamenta Rezzonico | Wed–Mon 10am–5pm, April–Oct until 6pm | carezzonico.visitmuve.it | stop: Ca' Rezzonico*

SANTA MARIA DELLA SALUTE (126 A–B5) (*∅ H9*)

This epitome of a Venetian Baroque church rises up in all its glory over the south-eastern end of the Canal Grande – a fantastic building, cloaked in white marble, designed by Baldassare Longhena on an octagonal layout. The church was erected in gratitude for an end to a plague epidemic and is crowned by a mighty dome that can be seen shining from far away. The vestry is decorated with altar

TIME TO CHILL

If you need a break from the cramped old town, take a trip across to the *Lido*. The narrow 12-km-/7.5-mi long island of sand that protects Venice and its lagoon from the open sea developed into a fashionable seaside resort towards the end of the 19th century, as those who have seen Luchino Visconti's film version of Thomas Mann's novella *Death in Venice* know. Today, things are much more down to earth here – except when film stars hold court in the Palazzo del Cinema during the International Film Festival. But the Lido has not lost any of its quality as a perfect place for sports enthusiasts and those just looking for the *dolce far niente*; with its flat, endless Adriatic beach that invites one to swim or go for a stroll, its countless pizzerias and ice cream parlours, it has something for everybody.

paintings by Titian, Tintoretto and other masters. *Daily 9am–noon and 3–5.30pm, vestry Mon–Sat 10am–noon and 3pm–5pm, Sun 3pm–5pm | stop: Salute*

PUNTA DELLA DOGANA
(126 B5) (*ɱ J9*)

The billionaire and patron of the arts François Pinault displays a representative overview of his unique collection here – including masterpieces by stars such as Jeff Koons, Richard Serra and Damien Hirst.

member of the upper class. To this day, the names on the bells of these elegant private homes read like a Who's Who of the global (moneyed) aristocracy. It's where the city's heart beats – and it's crammed with tourists.

But no matter how many backpacks bash into you, how many selfie sticks nearly have your eye out – the Piazza San Marco flashes; without it, you haven't seen Venice. So get into the Doge's Palace and Saint Mark's Basilica, and up the Campa-

Twenty-first century art in a palace of the Settecento: Martial Raysse at the Palazzo Grassi

The building that was erected as the former customs house at the eastern tip of Dorsoduro is crowned with two atlantes and a gilded globe of the world. *Wed–Mon 10am–7pm | joint ticket with Palazzo Grassi | www.palazzograssi.it | stop: Salute*

SAN MARCO

This district used to be the centre of power of the maritime republic. If you lived here, you were quite clearly a

nile! Them immerse yourself in the swirling masses in the alleys around the square, where an espresso at one of the tiny standing-only bars will cost a fraction of what you'd be charged at one of the famous coffee houses with their lace tablecloths, salons and orchestras on the actual square.

■ BASILICA DI SAN MARCO ★ ●
(126–127 C–D3) (*ɱ K7*)

Could it be more splendid? We think not. Five domes, lavishly decorated arches

The omnipresent Lion of St Mark is even on guard above the entrance to St Mark's Basilica

and windows, mosaics, icons, the high altar with St. Mark's sarcophagus, endless bronze figures – any other questions? The structure built in the form of a Greek cross in the 11th century, in which the relics that moulded Venice's identity – the bones of Saint Mark, stolen from Alexandria in Egypt – were once preserved, still forms its heart.

The main attractions: the incomparable stone mosaics that are, unfortunately, mostly covered by carpets; the sumptuously decorated, three-door iconostasis in the choir section (entrance with an extra ticket, to the right through the Capella di San Clemente), the high altar with the sarcophagus of Saint Mark, Sansovino's vestry door as well as his bronze figures, and the most precious treasure – the *Pala d'Oro* – a gold and enamel reredos with hundreds of precious stones created between the 10th and 14th centuries. And, of course, the magnificent *mosaics*: they illustrate episodes from the Old and New Testaments and cover an area of more than 43,000 ft². If you want to make a close inspection of them you should climb up to the gallery from the inner main portal. The *Tesoro*, the treasury, stores the most valuable collection of Byzantine silver and gold in the world (here, as with the Pala d'Oro, you also have to pay a small extra admission fee). Most of it came from Constantinople after the Venetians plundered it in 1204. Although much of it was seized by Napoleon and melted down, the *Tesoro* still has an impressive collection of liturgical objects, reliquaries and carvings. The *Museo Marciano* that has been established on the gallery above the vestibule is also well worth visiting. Along with priceless liturgical objects, it houses the Quadriga – four world-famous bronze horses that were probably cast in Ancient Rome.

Last but not least, there are the dazzling mosaics that were applied to the walls, arches and domes of the basilica over 800 years and which will certainly turn the visitor's head in more ways than one. They show scenes from the Old Testament (in the vestibule) and New (in the three-nave interior). Highlights include the depiction of the Holy Ghost as a dove with the Twelve Apostles in the dome closest to the main entrance, the Arch of the Passion with motifs from

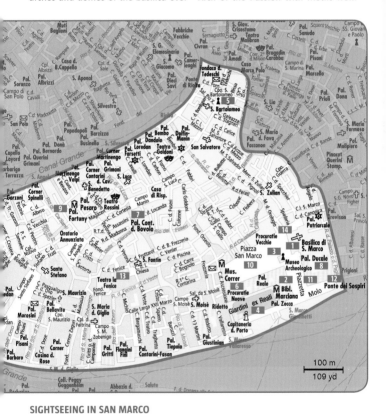

SIGHTSEEING IN SAN MARCO

1 Basilica di San Marco
2 Biblioteca Nazionale Marciana
3 Campanile di San Marco
4 Giardini ex Reali
5 Goldoni Memorial

6 Museo Correr
7 Palazzo Contarini del Bovolo
8 Palazzo Ducale
9 Palazzo Fortuny
10 Piazza San Marco

11 Piazzetta
12 Ponte dei Sospiri
13 Teatro La Fenice
14 Torre dell'Orologio

pre-Easter events, the Ascension Dome where the Saviour floats in a circle of stars supported by angels, and Christ as the blessing Pantocrator, as the „universal ruler", in the choir dome.

Admission is free on Sunday afternoons, but the queues are endless. If you want to save time rather than money, you can book an hour-long *Skip-the-Line Tour (21.50 euros | www.venetoinside.com)* of St. Mark's Basilica and all its treasures. Note: It is not permitted to take any kind of luggage into the church. Storage facilities at *Ateneo San Basso (Piazzetta dei Leoncini | daily from 9.30am–5.30pm). Basilica Mon–Sat 9.30am–5pm, Sun 2–4pm, until 5pm in summer; galleries daily from 9.45am–4.45pm; Pala d'Oro and Tesoro Mon–Sat 9.45am–4pm, Sun 2–4pm, until 5pm in summer | www.basilicasanmarco.it | stop: San Marco*

2 BIBLIOTECA NAZIONALE MARCIANA (126 C3) *(⚏ K8)*

Jacopo Sansovino was the Florentine architect who designed this monumental Renaissance construction. The main hall of what Palladio described as "possibly the most precious, richly-decorated building to be constructed since the days of the Ancient Greeks and Romans" is adorned with paintings by Veronese and Tintoretto, with the ceiling of the anteroom bearing a work by Titian. Among the most important of the approximately 900,000 volumes and 13,000 manuscripts are Marco Polo's last will and testament and the famous map of the world drawn by the monk Fra Mauro who once lived on Venice's cemetery island. *Entrance at the Museo Correr | Mon–Fri 8am–7pm, Sat 8am–1.30pm | joint ticket with Palazzo Ducale, Museo Correr and Museo Archeologico | www.marciana.veneziana.sbn.it | stop: Vallaresso*

3 CAMPANILE DI SAN MARCO ★ ☼ (126 C3) *(⚏ K8)*

It's an easy ride up this famous tower in a lift, from which eight daredevils announced in 1997 that Venice was splitting from the rest of Italy – an act of folly that earned them tremendous applause and a lawsuit. Fabulous views of the rooftops of Venice are guaranteed. The panorama not only provides you with a first, extremely helpful orientation aid but also a feeling for the unique location and structure of the city on the lagoon. The symbol of the city was originally erected in the 10th century and considerably increased in height in the 12th. The almost 100 m/328 ft high tower collapsed in 1902 but was reconstructed using the original material as much as possible. While queuing to buy tickets, you will have the opportunity to admire the Loggetta, built by Jacopo Sansovino around

1540. Venice's nobility used to like to gather for a chat under its arcades that form an architectural counterpart to the Scala dei Giganti ("Giants' Staircase") in the Doge's Palace opposite. *Easter–June and Oct daily 9am–7pm, July–Sept 9am–9pm, Nov–Easter 9.30am–3.45pm | stop: San Marco*

4 GIARDINI EX REALI
(126 C3–4) (*ᗰ J–K8*)

The only oasis of green in the stony heart of the city – and a very small one at that. Not a bad place to sit down on a shady bench to get your breath back. *Stop: San Marco*

5 GOLDONI MEMORIAL
(126 B–C1) (*ᗰ J6*)

Even cast in bronze, Carlo Goldoni, Venice's great comedy playwright, seems to be smiling to himself. This is not surprising seeing that the *Campo San Bartolomeo* where the statue is located is especially popular with the Venetians as a place to come and gossip or share a drink until late at night. The charming statue was created in 1883 by the Venetian Antonio dal Zotto. *Stop: Rialto*

6 MUSEO CORRER
(126 B–C3) (*ᗰ J8*)

This city museum with its incredibly rich collections, which is located in the Napoleon Wing and Procuratie Nuove, behind the south-west façade of the Piazza San Marco, invites you to take a journey to the roots of Venetian (art) history. The neo-Classicist rooms on the first floor display some early works by the renowned sculptor Antonio Canova and a comprehensive overview of the major historical themes of the city on the lagoon ranging from trade and seafaring or politics, administration and war history to the arts, trade and festivities. Official robes and

magnificent vestments worn by dignitaries are on display along with coins and the marble Lions of Saint Mark, old maritime and land maps as well as the first detailed plan of the city created by Jacopo de' Barbari around 1500. One additional focus of attention is the documentation of Venetian history from the end

Eye-catcher: the Campanile di San Marco

of the Republic in 1797 to the unification of the city with the Kingdom of Italy in the 1860s. After ten years of restoration work, the re-opened INSIDER TIP imperial chambers, in which the Empress Sisi, the wife of the Hapsburg Emperor Franz Joseph, resided for a total of eight months during two trips to the city, are a new attraction at the museum.

A large section of the second floor is reserved for the picture gallery: precious paintings and sculptures from the Veneto-Byzantine and early-Gothic periods, into the Cinquecento, the golden 16th century. The highlights include works by Jacopo Bellini and his family, their contemporaries as well as Lorenzo Lotto who was active one generation later and the snow-white marble statues created by Antonio Canova. The most famous exhibit in the museum by far, however, is Vittorio Carpaccio's picture of two "Venetian Ladies" painted around 1510 that supposedly shows two smug courtesans with their dogs and birds. *Summer daily 10am–7pm, winter 10am–5pm | joint ticket with Palazzo Ducale, Biblioteca Marciana and Museo Archeologico | correr. visitmuve.it | stop: Vallaresso*

7 PALAZZO CONTARINI DEL BOVOLO
(126 B2–3) (*ω H7*)

If you follow a small yellow sign on the south side of Campo Marin and go around two or three corners, you will find yourself in front of this example of playful Renaissance architecture. The "Snail Shell", INSIDER TIP a spiral staircase with elegant arcades erected around 1500, winds its way upwards on the façade of the noble Contarini family's Gothic palace. *Daily 10am–1.30pm and 2pm–4pm | www. scalabovolo.org | stop: Rialto, Sant'Angelo*

8 PALAZZO DUCALE ★ ●
(127 D3) (*ω K8*)

The most palatial of all palaces; a centre of political and legislative power, the greatest symbol of Venetian civilisation. Over the past 1000 years, 120 doges guided the destiny of the Sea Republic from within its walls. In the Gothic form we see today, most of the complex,

which consists of three wings between 70 and 100 m/230 and 330 ft in length, was constructed in the 14th and early 15th centuries.

The colossal marble façade, whose lower section is interspersed with countless delicate columns and arches, deserves our greatest admiration. Take a closer look at the wonderful sculptures of "Adam and Eve" and "Drunken Noah" on the corners of the south wing, as well as the scenes on each one of the capitals of the dozens of columns! A tour of the interior of the Doge's Palace is completely overwhelming. It begins at the high-Gothic main portal, the Porta della Carta, opposite the Loggetta and Campanile. You pass through it to enter the inner court that is dominated by a two-storey triumphal arch, the *Arco Foscari*, and the *Scala dei Giganti* watched over by two statues, one of Neptune and one of Mars, created by Jacopo Sansavino.

The greatest Italian painters of the 16th century were involved in decorating the rooms; the most important were Tintoretto, Titian and Paolo Veronese. Most of the gigantic pictures they painted show scenes from the history of the city, from the myths surrounding its foundation to great military victories. However, the greatest impression is probably made by the *Sala del Maggior Consiglio*, a hall measuring 54 × 25 m (177.2 × 82 ft) where as many as 1800 members of the Grand Council met to elect high state officials and the members of the Signoria. Your eyes will be drawn towards Tintoretto's painting of Paradise on the end wall; at 7 × 22 m (23 × 72.2 ft) it is the largest painting on canvas in the world. The tour ends with a walk over the Bridge of Sighs to the New Prison.

The guided tours on "secret paths", *Itinerari Segreti*, which are held in Italian, French and English, are very special. Tickets can be bought at the information desk at the palace entrance or online at least 48 hours in advance (visit to the palace is included in the ticket price). You will be able to visit the false ceiling of the Hall of the Great Council, the offices of the Grand Chancellor, the secret archives and the notorious "lead chambers" (*piombi*) where Giacomo Casanova was once incarcerated. *Daily 8.30am–6pm, April–Oct until 7pm | joint ticket with Biblioteca Marciana, Museo Correr and Museo Archeologico | palazzoducale.visit muve.it | stop: San Zaccaria*

9 PALAZZO FORTUNY
(126 A2) (*∅ H7*)

The Spanish-born painter Mariano Fortuny lived for more than 40 years in this Gothic palazzo. The highly-gifted artist worked as a painter, sculptor, stage

The power and splendour of the city republic unfolds before your eyes in the Doge's Palace

designer, lighting technician, decorator and also designed magnificent silk fabrics and hand-painted lamps. The building has been totally renovated and now documents all of the facets of the work and collecting activities of this astounding personality. There are interesting temporary exhibitions on the ground floor. *Calle Pesaro 3958 | Wed–Mon 10am–6pm | fortuny.visitmuve.it | stop: Sant'Angelo*

🔟 PIAZZA SAN MARCO ⭐
(126 C3) (*𝄜 J–K 7–8*)

Napoleon's exclamation that this is "the most beautiful salon on earth" is still valid more than two hundred years later. The 175 m/574 ft long, slightly trapezoid-shaped St Mark's Square is really unique and conjures up a different atmosphere depending on the time of day and season. It has been the site of countless religious processions and a great number of very earthly festivities. The Piazza has remained a stage for the vanity of both locals and tourists alike to this very day. And, during those rare hours on foggy winter days or late at night when the usual masses have deserted it and it finally comes to rest, isolated dreamers will find it a magical setting. The buildings around this square that was first laid out more than 800 years ago are described separately in this chapter. Here, we can only recommend that you do what generations of travellers before you have done, stroll through the arcades with their luxury shops and across the square and inhale the atmosphere of this unique setting. *Stop: San Marco*

🔟🔟 PIAZZETTA (126–127 C–D3) (*𝄜 K8*)

The elongated area between the Campanile and Canale di San Marco, flanked on the east by the Doge's Palace and on the west by the Biblioteca Marciana, has fulfilled many functions over the centuries. For a period, gambling took place

In the *sestiere* of Castello you will still find the "everyday" Venice with corner shops *alla veneziana*

here in the open air, market stalls were set up, as were latrines, and public executions also took place here. Now it is a meeting place for people on a stroll through the city and souvenir sellers. All of these activities are watched over by Venice's first patron saint Theodor – accompanied by his crocodile – and a winged Lion of Saint Mark on top of two massive columns. *Stop: San Marco*

12 PONTE DEI SOSPIRI
(127 D3) (🛱 K8)

You will almost imagine that you can still hear the sighs of the prisoners who once made their way, protected from any curious onlookers, over this draughty corridor from the courtroom in the Doge's Palace to the New Prison *(Palazzo delle Prigioni)*. But, only almost, because the incessant chatter of the hordes of tourists and the clicking of the cameras shooting away at the Bridge of Sighs from the Ponte della Paglia on the quay drown out everything. *Stop: San Zaccaria*

13 TEATRO LA FENICE ⭐
(126 A3) (🛱 H8)

It's hard to believe that this classical theatre is a fake. The plush red seats, the stucco, the gold – everything looks as if it dates back to the 18th century. But sadly, this world-famous opera house burnt down in 1996 and had to be rebuilt. The decision was made to rebuild it to look exactly like the original – and so it was! Even if you don't like opera, just pop in and enjoy the atmosphere! *Campo San Fantin 1965 | daily 9.30am–6pm | www.teatrolafenice.it | stop: Giglio*

14 TORRE DELL'OROLOGIO
(CLOCK TOWER) 🔄 (126 C3) (🛱 K7)

With its blue and white façade, crowned with a Lion of Saint Mark and the large dial, the clock tower designed by Mauro Codussi sometime around 1500 marks the spot where the Mercerie enters the Piazza di San Marco. From the roof terrace, two bronze giants deafeningly strike the hour. You need to book in advance if you would like to go up *(tel. 0 41 42 73 08 92)* as part of a guided tour *(in Italian: daily at 12 noon and 4pm, in English Mon–Wed 10am and 11am, Thu–Sun 12 noon and 3pm). Piazza San Marco | stop: San Marco*

CASTELLO

The largest of the six municipal districts – and the one with the most contrasts: immediately behind the Doge's Palace and along the Riva Degli Schiavoni, there is the hustle and bustle of tourist life and a row of luxury hotels next to each other, but a little further east, around Via Garibaldi and in the winding streets where the shipyard workers used to live, it is much more intimate.

Small workshops, stores, narrow streets with clotheslines overhead and children playing: this is where Venice shows its friendly, everyday – occasionally a little impoverished – side. But, there are also many artistic treasures waiting to be discovered here too – churches such as San Zaccaria and Santi Giovanni e Paolo with the doges' graves, or the scuole of the Dalmatians and Greeks. The largest green area in the city, the Giardini Pubblici, will give you a chance to catch a breath of fresh air. This is where the Biennale, a show of what is happening in the world of contemporary art, is held every two years.

The shipyard, the Arsenale, is a deserted alien element that, even today, is absolutely off-limits to the unauthorised.

A pack of lions guard the gate at the entrance to the Arsenale

1 ARSENALE
(128–129 B–D 1–3) (*M N–P 6–8*)

This shipyard, where Venice built all the ships for its gigantic navy and merchant fleet, and where weapons and gunpowder were also stored, was the centre of the largest sea power in the Eastern Mediterranean from the 14th to the late 18th century and consequently heavily guarded. Today, ferries and freighters are repaired in the 79 acres area with its magnificent entrance (*Ingresso di Terra*) flanked by four lions. This is also the site of several high-tech companies, workshops and offices. Today, the Italian military forces still preside over a small section. That is why the northern part of the arsenal recently stopped being a prohibited military area and is now open to the public. In summer, the Italian Navy offers INSIDER TIP evening guided tours of the southern part. To go along, please book by email no later than 4pm on the previous day (*maristudi@marina.difesa.it*). As the arsenals are also the headquarters of the company that is responsible for the MOSE flood protection project, you can also book guided tours of the vast lock construction here (email *info@mose-venezia.it*). Mon–Fri 9am–6pm | *arsenale.comune.venezia.it* | *stop: Arsenale*

2 BARBARIA DE LE TOLE
(127 E1) (*M L–M6*)

This tranquil alley used to resound with carpentering and hammering from dawn to dusk. It was home and workplace to craftsman who sold their *tole* (wood panels) to countries as far away as Arabia. Although the trade eventually died out, the carpenters' street remained with their *botteghe*. The white Renaissance church of *Santa Maria dei Derelitti* is very pretty. Do not miss it! *Stop: Ospedale*

3 CAMPO DE LE GATE
(127 F2) (*M N7*)

This quiet little square is magical. Just sit and be still for a moment. Perhaps you are familiar with some of the works by the poet Ugo Foscolo? There is a memorial plaque to the Italian writer, who lived here for a few years. *Stop: San Zaccaria*

4 CAMPO DI SANTA MARIA FORMOSA
(127 D1) (*M K–L6*)

Theatre performances, festivals and bullfights used to be held here on one of the largest and most beautiful squares in Venice. These spectacles, however, are all things of the past. But this is still a great

place to have an ice cream or cup of coffee and watch everyday life go by around the rather isolated Santa Maria Formosa Church – by Venetian standards. *Stop: San Zaccaria*

5 GIARDINI PUBBLICI
(128–129 C–D 5–6) (⨕ P9–10)

Great for a stroll through greenery. As you might imagine, you won't see much in the way of grass or lines of trees in Venice. And the *Serra*, the glasshouse of 1894, has a ⓦ *Caffetteria (daily from 10am–8pm).* It serves sweet and savoury snacks, all organic. A very relaxed atmosphere at cocktail time. V*iale Garibaldi 1254 | www.serra deigiardini.org | stop: Giardini*

6 INSIDER TIP MUSEO QUERINI STAMPALIA *(127 D2) (⨕ L7)*

The collection of paintings is the highlight of any tour of this splendid patrician's house. It includes works by Giovanni Bellini, Palma il Vecchio and Giambattista Tiepolo, as well as the genre scenes of everyday life in Venice by Pietro Longhi and Gabriele Bella. The tour through a total of 20 rooms is especially fascinating because it will give you an idea of the magnificent surroundings the wealthy nobility of the 18th century, like Count Querini Stampilia, lived in. They would socialise beneath opulent ceiling frescos, Rococo stucco and chandeliers made of Murano glass, between magnificent mirrors, lacquer furniture and the walls of the library with a whopping 200,000 books on its shelves. *Tue–Sun 10am–6pm | www.querinistampalia.it | stop: San Zaccaria*

7 MUSEO STORICO NAVALE
(128 B4) (⨕ N–O8)

The Museum of Naval History is fittingly housed in an old warehouse right next to the Arsenal and covers the history of the maritime republic from the perspective of shipping. There are many models of battle and passenger ships, canons from five centuries, explanations of how gondolas and fortresses are built, as well as fishing nets, nautical charts, navigational equipment and pious votive pictures testifying to miraculous rescues at sea. The highlight is definitely the "Bucintoro", the state galley from which the doge performed the annual "Marriage of the Sea" ritual. An ● INSIDER TIP extra tour through the Ships Pavilion, a huge collection of historic vessels, is worthwhile. At the time we went to press, the museum was closed for refurbishment. However, you can visit the

The highlight in the Museo Storico Navale: the golden Bucintoro

Pavilion of Ships *(Padiglione delle Navi | daily 8.45am–5pm)* at the Ponte dell' Arsenale via the Rio della Tana. *www.visit muve.it | stop: Arsenale*

🔳8 SAN FRANCESCO DELLA VIGNA (128 A1) *(𝄞 N6)*

Place of pilgrimage for lovers of architecture. This convent on the grounds of a former vineyard *(vigna)* is more like an ancient temple. That is thanks to the person who built it: Andrea Palladio was *the* star architect of the Renaissance. The classicist villas he designed for the Venetian nobility are world-famous. Here he "pimped up" a place of worship. *Daily 8am–12 and 3pm–7pm | stop: Celestia*

🔳9 SANTI GIOVANNI E PAOLO (123 D–E6) *(𝄞 L5)*

The importance official Venice attached to the Dominicans as the order that commissioned this house of worship can be seen by the fact that no fewer than 27 doges have found their final resting places here. The graves gife a lesson in how the local art of sculpture developed from the late-Gothic to the Baroque periods. Its colossal high point is at the grave of Alvise Mocenigo by the inner church portal. The Baroque altar opposite it, designed by Baldassare Longhena, is hardly any less massive. The overall impression of the interior of this mendicant order's church is conspicuously ascetic but it is enhanced by some magnificent works of art including paintings by Giovanni Bellini, Lorenzo Lotto and Paolo Veronese. Take a closer look at the Renaissance façade of the immediately adjacent *Scuola Grande di San Marco* with its wonderful reliefs and marble intarsia. *Mon–Sat 9am–6pm, Sun noon–6pm, please note: these times change frequently | stop: Ospedale*

🔳10 SAN ZACCARIA (127 E3) *(𝄞 L7)*

The marble façade of this church only two or three minutes' walk from the Doge's Palace is a real feast for the eyes and there are several important artworks inside, including one of Giovanni Bellini's most important paintings, the beautiful Sacra Conversazione (Maria with Child). The campanile was part of the former

SPOTLIGHTS ON SPORTS

The city on the lagoon offers rowing fans an unforgettable spectacle that is absolutely unique worldwide: every year, on a Sunday mostly at the end of May, Venice comes under the spell of the ⭐ *Vogalonga*, a 30 km/18.6 mi rowing marathon with more than 5000 amateur participants leaning into the oars. The more than 1500 vessels – all classes, from canoe and gondola, to rowing and dragon boats are allowed – create a tremendously colourful picture and great fun is had by all. The route starts at the Bacino San Marco and takes the rowers all the way to Burano and back to the *centro storico* by way of Murano. The most popular places to watch the spectacle are the Riva degli Schiavoni, the main canal in Murano, Canal di Cannaregio and the Canal Grande. Around half of the participants come from abroad. Anybody with a boat and enough muscle power can take part. Information and registration: *tel. 04 15 21 05 44 | www.vogalonga.it*

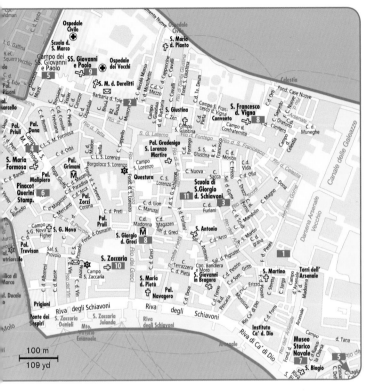

SIGHTSEEING IN CASTELLO

1 Arsenale
2 Barbaria de le Tole
3 Campo de le Gate
4 Campo di Santa Maria Formosa

5 Giardini Pubblici
6 Museo Querini Stampalia
7 Museo Storico Navale
8 San Francesco della Vigna

9 Santi Giovanni e Paolo
10 San Zaccaria
11 Scuola di San Giorgio degli Schiavoni

church erected in the 12th century and this makes it one of the oldest bell towers in Venice. *Mon–Sat 10am–noon and 4pm–6pm, Sun 4pm–6pm, please note: these times change frequently | stop: San Zaccaria*

11 SCUOLA DI SAN GIORGIO DEGLI SCHIAVONI (127 F2) (Ø M7)
The brotherhood of the Slavonic people was founded in 1452 by wealthy Dalmatian merchants with the aim of supporting impoverished, old seamen from their homeland and providing education for their children. The small oratory is one of the few rooms in the city where the paintings are still surrounded by their original carved and gilded panelling. Its greatest treasure is the cycle of paintings created at the beginning of the 16th

One of the four synagogues in the ghetto is the Scuola Levantina

century by Vittore Carpaccio. It shows scenes from the life of the patron saints of Dalmatia – George, Trifon and Hieronymus – painted with the elegance so typical of this artist. *Mon 2.45–6pm, Tue–Sat 9.15am–1pm and 2.45–6pm, Sun 9.15am–1pm | stop: San Zaccaria*

CANNAREGIO

The north-west district between the station and the Rialto Bridge is, on the one hand, very touristy because it's where everyone tries to push through to St. Mark's Square, but on the other hand it's also the most densely populated, with only a few second homes belonging to wealthy foreigners. It includes 33 islands and lots of canals.

There are some wonderful walks along these canals. There are some lovely restaurants away from the city's main artery (Lista di Spagna/Rio Terà San Leonardo/Strada Nova), with terraces by the water, and bars, where the locals like to come for a quick espresso. And there are numerous breathtaking palazzi on the northern shores of the Canal Grande. Be sure to visit the former Jewish Ghetto as well, which is in the middle of Cannaregio. Lovely synagogues and kosher restaurants radiate an entirely unique atmosphere.

■ CHIESA DEI GESUITI
(122 C4) (*ω K3–4*)

A little bit off the usual tourist track, on the north-eastern border of Cannaregio, a classic example of Venetian high-Baroque architecture rises into the sky: the main church of the Jesuit Order that was not always warmly welcomed in St Mark's Republic. The façade, with its colossal columns and elaborate sculptural decoration, creates a striking first impression. The painstakingly renovated interior, with its shades of green and white, is even more impressive. Your eyes will be drawn towards the elaborate high altar designed by Giuseppe Pozzo. The most precious decoration, however, is Titian's expressive painting of the torture of St Laurentius in the first chapel of the left-hand nave. *Campo dei Gesuiti | Mon–Fri 10am–noon and 4–7pm, in winter 10am–6pm | stop: Fondamenta Nove*

2 GHETTO (121 E3) (*𝄞 F2–3*)

Located in the centre of Cannaregio, this "district within a district" has the rather dubious honour of having served as a kind of model for all the ghettos created later throughout the world. At the beginning of the 16th century, the Senate allocated this district to be the home of the 5000 members of the very successful and influential Jewish community. This area, whose name comes from the metal foundries – the *getti* – that were formerly located here, was conveniently surrounded by canals. Gates were added and manned by – Christian – guards, and blocks of flats were built that were rented to Jews at exorbitant rates. The names of the three sections are misleading; the "new" Ghetto Nuovo is actually 25 years older than the "old" Ghetto Vecchio. The "newest" Ghetto Nuovissimo was created when the area was extended around 1630.

The four magnificent synagogues in the Ghetto are well worth visiting: the *Scuola La Tedesca* built in 1528 by German Ashkenazi Jews, the four year younger *Scuola Canton* that is now in the Rococo style, the *Scuola Levantina* from the sec-

ond half of the 17th century with its splendidly carved pulpit by Andrea Brustolon and the largest *Scuola Spagnola* that is especially impressive on account of the use of multi-coloured marble. The very informative guided tours also include a visit to the *Museo Ebraico (Sun–Fri – except on Jewish holidays – 10am–7pm, winter 10am–5.30pm | www. museoebraico.it)* where precious torah shrines, silver candelabras, documents, textiles, furniture and musical instruments bring the rich tradition of Venice's Jewish community back to life. *Tours Sun–Fri (except on Jewish holidays) in Italian and English every hour 10.30am–5.30pm (winter until 4.30pm) | meeting place at the Museum | stop: Guglie*

3 MADONNA DELL'ORTO (122 A2) (*𝄞 H2*)

An artistic jewel that is unjustly neglected: the brick façade of this Gothic church in the north with its statues of the Apostles and finely carved windows is a feast for the eyes. And there are a number of INSIDER TIP top class paintings inside, including John the Baptist by Cima da Conegliano and several works by Tintoretto, who is buried in the apse. *Mon–Sat 10am–5pm, Sun noon–5pm | stop: Madonna dell'Orto*

4 INSIDER TIP SANTA MARIA DEI MIRACOLI (122 C6) (*𝄞 K5*)

Fortunately, this pretty Renaissance church was restored in the 1990s! Now its unusual façade with the multi-coloured marble panels can once again be seen at its best. Nor is the inside without a „wow!" effect: the precious filigree stone masonry that is seen throughout the interior is a real eye-catcher. *Mon 10.30am–4pm, Tue–Sat 10.30am–4.30pm | stop: Rialto*

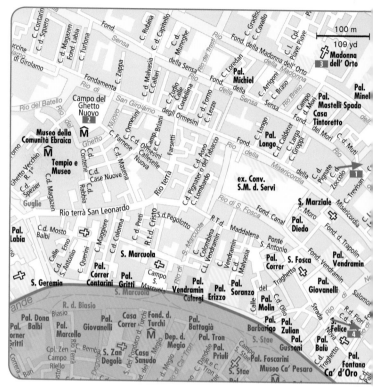

SIGHTSEEING IN CANNAREGIO

- **1** Chiesa dei Gesuiti
- **2** Ghetto
- **3** Madonna dell'Orto
- **4** Santa Maria dei Miracoli

SAN POLO & SANTA CROCE

The city started to grow from this core area west of Rialto Bridge more than 1000 years ago.

The old trading and banking district on the Canal Grande has hardly lost any of its former bustling activity: the many shops, the fish, fruit and vegetable markets make a stroll around here a feast for the senses. The many palaces and churches, with Santa Maria Gloriosa dei Frari in first place, and the neighbouring Scuola Grande di San Rocco also make it an important hunting ground for art lovers. The best place to watch this hive of activity over a cappuccino or *ombra* – a small glass of wine – is on Campo San Polo, the second largest open space in the city, or in the area between Pescheria and Rialto where many chic shops have breathed new life into the area.

◼1 CAMPO SAN GIACOMO DELL'ORIO ● (121 E5–6) (𝒫 F5)

A small, quiet place with trees: quite a rarity in Venice! Have a look inside the church INSIDER TIP *San Giacomo dell'Orio (Mon 10.30am–4pm, Tue–Sat 10.30am–4.30pm)*. After all, it was founded in the 9th century, and then extended several times, always in the style of the prevailing art period at the time. The result is an amusing hotch-potch of styles. Then perhaps a glass of wine? In good weather, the *Al Prosecco (closed Sun)* wine bar sets up tables outside – lovely!

◼2 CAMPO SAN POLO (125 F1–2) (𝒫 G6)

This square is vast, and perfect for a rest – whether free of charge on one of the benches, or over a drink at one of the pretty street cafés. *Stop: San Silvestro*

◼3 CASA GOLDONI (125 E2) (𝒫 G6–7)

The birthplace of playwright Carlo Goldoni, Italy's 18th century answer to, possibly, Richard Bean. People roared with laughter at his comedies based on the skinflint Pantalone and his scatterbrained manservant Arlecchino. However, his writing did not make his fortune, and he had to supplement it by working as a lawyer. Later on, he became an Italian teacher at the French court, which should have set him up for life – had it not been for the French Revolution. Goldoni, who is today considered the first representative of modern Italian theatre, died in poverty in Paris. *Calle dei Nomboli 2793 | Thu–Tue 10am–4pm | carlogoldoni.visitmuve.it | stop: San Tomà*

◼4 FRARI ★ (125 E2) (𝒫 F6)

Along with the Dominican church of Santi Giovanni e Paolo, the "Frari", as Santa Maria Gloriosa dei Frari is called for short, is the second largest Gothic church of the mendicant order in the city. In contrast with their self-imposed humility and the building's modest exterior, its commissioners, the Franciscans, did not hide their light under a bushel in the interior. The first thing you will notice in the enormous nave is the pyramidal tomb of Antonio Canova with Titian's grave and his Pesaro Madonna opposite. There are precious altarpieces by Bartolomeo Vivarini and Giovanni Bellini, as well as a statue of St John by Donatello in the choir chapels and sacristy where the composer Claudio Monteverdi is also buried.

However, the most fascinating eye-catcher is the painting above the high altar. Titian's floating Assunta (Ascension of the Virgin Mary) was a stroke of genius on the part of the artist; its incredible

A visit to the „Richard Bean of the 18th century": Casa Goldoni

colouration and composition, striving dramatically upwards towards the heavens, were something completely new at the end of the Renaissance and already point towards the Baroque. *Mon–Sat 9am–6pm, Sun 1–6pm | stop: San Tomà*

◾5 PALAZZO MOCENIGO
(121 F5) (*G4–5*)

Located directly behind Ca' Pesaro and San Stae Church, this magnificent early-17th century palace, with its furniture,

chandeliers, textiles and other decorative objects, gives a good idea of the luxury in which the nobility of the period liked to indulge. A study centre for the history of textiles and fashion has been established in some of its stately rooms; its library can also be visited by those who are interested. *Palace Tue–Sun 10am–5pm (winter until 4pm), Study Centre and Library Tue and Thu 8.30am–5pm, Wed and Fri 8.30am–1.30pm | stop: San Stae*

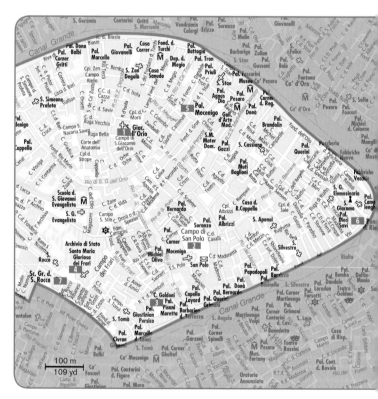

SIGHTSEEING IN SAN POLO & SANTA CROCE

◾1 Chiesa dei Gesuiti
◾2 Campo San Polo
◾3 Casa Goldoni
◾4 Frari
◾5 Palazzo Mocenigo
◾6 Ponte di Rialto
◾7 Scuola Grande di San Rocco

Over or under it: the Rialto Bridge is a must

6 PONTE DI RIALTO ★
(126 B1) (*ω J6*)

Hard-working statisticians have counted that more than 400 bridges help one cross the around 150 canals in Venice and join many of the more than 100 islands. Some are unnamed, some rather nondescript. Others play an important role for traffic or are of special artistic interest, or have become popular as meeting places – or world-famous photo motifs such as Rialto Bridge. For centuries, this site was the centre of business in the trading metropolis of Venice. It was here that merchants unloaded their goods from faraway lands and the most important banks and trading companies set up their offices.

In its present form, the bridge joining the sestieri of San Marco and San Polo was constructed using stone from Istria at the end of the 16th century to replace its rotting, wooden predecessor. Until the middle of the 19th century, it was the only way for pedestrians to cross the Canal Grande. Its architect was a certain Antonio da Ponte whose – not especially elegant, but solid – design, allowing sufficient room for boats to pass beneath it, won against competitors of the ilk of Michelangelo, Palladio, Sansovino and Scamozzi. *Stop: Rialto*

7 SCUOLA GRANDE DI SAN ROCCO
(125 D2) (*ω E–F6*)

Someone not struck dumb by the treasures in this meeting house is probably not moved by any form of art at all! The walls and ceilings of this building dedicated to Saint Roch, who gave protection from the Plague, are decorated with no fewer than 56 paintings, created over a period of 18 years in the late 16th century by Jacopo Robusti, better known as Tintoretto. They show scenes from the Old and New Testaments. With its perfect proportions and magnificent panelled ceiling, the main hall on the upper floor is considered one of the most exquisite rooms in all of Italy. The adjacent hostel (*Sala dell'Albergo*) with Tintoretto's *Crucifixion* of 1565 is hardly any less impressive. The eight large-format paintings of the life of the Virgin Mary in the – rather gloomy – entrance hall on the ground floor are also well worth seeing. A few years ago, the *Scoletta di San Rocco (daily 9.30am–6pm)* opposite the *scuola grande* opened its doors to visitors. It is quite charming but considerably more modestly decorated and is now used for interesting temporary exhibitions. On no account should you miss *San Rocco Church (daily 9.30am–5.30pm)* next door with its magnificent Tintoretto paintings. *Daily 9.30am–5.30pm | www.scuola grandesanrocco.it | stop: San Tomà*

DORSODURO

Venice's "strong backbone", the *sestiere* in the south-west of the old town, presents itself as a charming mixture of rustic provinciality (during the day) and – thanks to the university nearby – student dynamism (in the evening) on its main square, Campo Santa Margherita, and in its side streets.

The proletarian traditions of the city can be seen and felt on its outskirts, especially on the island of Giudecca to the south and in the west near the harbour – and both areas are part of Dorsoduro. Some parts of the abandoned industrial areas look grim, others as if they were being prepared for different purposes. Venice is also undergoing structural change, and there is a crea-

tive scene that needs space. It has it here.
● *Zattere*, the promenade along the Giudecca Canal, is the perfect place to take in some sun in winter. The view across the water to Palladio's churches is an absolute dream. Art lovers' hearts will start to beat faster further to the east, between the Accademia, the Guggenheim Gallery and Santa Maria della Salute. It is definitely worth making a detour to the monastery island of San Giorgio Maggiore, not only to admire the fantastic panoramic view from the campanile (read more about it in the Palladio walk in the "Discovery Tours" chapter).

■ CAMPO SANTA MARGHERITA
(125 D3) (∅ E7)

The long, narrow main square of the Dorsoduro sestiere offers a strange mixture: on the one hand, its is probably Venice's most folksy campo – with a fish and vegetable market, wine bars and an everyday lifestyle similar to that in a village. On the other, it is in the centre of an extremely lively youth and student scene that has developed in recent years with countless bars, pubs and cabaret theatres between Campo San Pantalon in the north and Rio di San Barnaba in the south.

The Carmelite order's church of *Santa Maria del Carmine (Mon–Sat 7am–noon and 2.30–7pm)*, mostly just called Carmini, and its *Scuola Grande dei Carmine (daily 11am–5pm)*, decorated with paintings by Giambattista Tiepolo, form the south-west end of the Campo. A beautiful Adoration of the Shepherds by Cima da Congeliano (in the second wall altar) and Lorenzo Lotto's St Nicholas above the opposite altar can be admired behind the brick façade and threateningly skew-whiff baroque campanile. There are also performances of INSIDER TIP ▶ operas in period costumes several times a week *(www.musicain maschera.it). Stops: San Basilio, Ca' Rezzonico*

2 COLLEZIONE PEGGY GUGGENHEIM ● (125 F5) (⟰ G9)

Cubism and Surrealism, Action Painting and abstract art – there is no movement in classical modern art that Peggy Guggenheim, a rich heiress and patron of the arts, did not collect in her Palazzo Venier dei Leoni. The low building has become a mecca for lovers of 20th-century art. Among the great painters and sculptors on display here are Joan Mirò,

Wed–Mon 10am–6pm | www.guggenheim-venice.it | stop: Accademia, Salute

3 GALLERIA DELL'ACCADEMIA ★ ● (125 E5) (⟰ F9)

Bellini, Carpaccio, Giorgione, Tintoretto, Titian and Veronese, Canaletto, Guardi, Longhi, Mantegna, Lotto, Piazzetta and Tiepolo... There is hardly a single prominent representative of the more than 500-year history of Venetian painting who has not found a place in this museum on the southern bank of the Canal Grande. It is no wonder that this art gallery is considered one of the most im-

The Ponte del Pugni spans over the Rio di San Barnaba in Dorsoduro

René Magritte, Henri Matisse, Henry Moore, Piet Mondrian, Wassily Kandinsky, Georges Braque, Paul Klee, Jackson Pollock and many, many more. The museum shop sells fabulous posters and art books, writing accessories and postcards – it's a great place to browse!

portant in the world. Don't be put off by the long queues of visitors that sometimes line up in front of the neo-Classicist façade: it is well worth being patient and waiting to see what is on display in the two dozen rooms of the spacious complex of buildings that was developed

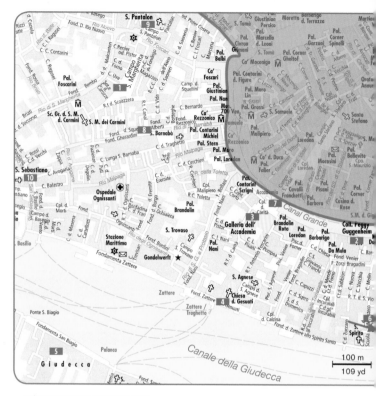

SIGHTSEEING IN DORSODURO

1 Campo Santa Margherita
2 Collezione Peggy Guggenheim
3 Galleria dell'Accademia
4 Gesuati
5 Giudecca
6 Magazzini del Sale
7 Ponte dell'Accademia
8 Ponte dei Pugni
9 San Pantalon
10 San Sebastiano

out of the former church, monastery and Scuola della Carità. If you do not want to wait too long, you can book in advance for a fixed time *(tel. 04 15 20 03 45)* at an extra charge of 1.50 euros. If you don't want to spend half a day in the museum, have a look at the following highlights: several Madonnas painted by Giovanni Bellini, Gentile Bellini's "Miracle of the Relic of the Cross", Vit-

tore Carpaccio's "Legend of St Ursula" cycle, Giorgione's "The Tempest" and "Old Woman", various Old Testament scenes and portraits of saints by Tintoretto and Paolo Veronese, as well as scenes of everyday life by Pietro Longhi, landscapes and views of cities by Canaletto and Francesco Guardi. And finally, Tiziano Vecellio, alias Titian: this giant among the masters of the Renaissance is represented with a wonderful painting of "John the Baptist", his last work, "Pietà", and "The Presentation of the Virgin Mary", the only painting by Titian that is still in the place it was intended for. *Tue–Sun 8.15am–7.15pm, Mon 8.15am–2pm | www.galleriaaccademia. org | stop: Accademia*

◼4 GESUATI (125 E6) (*𝄞 F9*)

On your stroll along the picturesque Zattere quay, it is worth taking some time to visit this sacred building designed by the great Venetian architect of the Baroque period, Giorgio Massari, to admire the beautiful ceiling frescos by Giambattista Tiepolo and altarpieces by Tintoretto, Giovanni Battista Piazzetta and Sebastiano Ricci. *Mon–Sat 10am–5pm | stop: Zattere*

◼5 GIUDECCA ★ ☼
(131 D4) (*𝄞 C–K 10–12*)

This island to the south of the old city is actually made up of eight smaller ones connected to each other. In the Middle Ages, this was the home of the Jews *guidei* (from which the name probably stems) who had been expelled from the city. Later, rich Venetians built their summer villas here, followed, in the 19th century, by trade and industry.

Today, the main reason for visiting this area of the city, which is under the administration of the Dorsoduro sestiere, is to see Palladio's two churches: Redentore and Zitelle. Well-heeled guests book into the five-star Cipriani Hotel on the eastern tip. The former Molino Stucky grain mill in the west, which partially burned down in 2003, has come back to life as a luxurious Hilton Hotel. *Stops: Zitelle, Redentore, Palanca*

◼6 MAGAZZINI DEL SALE
(126 A6) (*𝄞 H10*)

The newest and most modern museum in the district, housed in what was once a salt store. On display are works by the celebrated abstract expressionist Emilio Vedova, who died in 2006. As space is limited, architect Renzo Piano – who was a friend of Vedova – came up with

Magritte, Matisse, Miró, Mondrian and Modigliani: a mecca of modern art

An island skirting the
city of islands: Giudecca

porary replacement for its predecessor that was too low for *vaporetto* traffic. But, as is often the case with interim solutions, the Venetians have become used to it and no longer want to be without it when they – and all of the visitors from far and near – admire the wonderful view down the canal towards Salute and, in the opposite direction, to Palazzo Balbi at the mouth of the Rio Foscari. *Stop: Accademia*

8 PONTE DEI PUGNI
(125 D4) (*Ш E8*)

Until a few years ago, this bridge at Campo San Barnaba was one of only a few without a railing. Now it is more difficult to fall off it into the Rio di San Barnaba it spans. And it's much longer since the end of the spectacle for which is is named: Bridge of Fists. Until into the 16th century, rival factions of the city fought with their fists atop the bridge. The winning team was the one that knocked its opponents off the bridge and into the water. *Stop: Ca' Rezzonico*

9 INSIDER TIP SAN PANTALON ●
(125 D2) (*Ш E7*)

A little-known sensation lies waiting behind this modest – or one could say, completely blank – façade: a gigantic ceiling painting made up of 40 individual canvas elements that will really turn your head in more ways than one. Gian Antonio Fumiani was the man who worked for 24 years (!) to create this colossal Baroque work at the end of the 17th century. *Mon–Sat 10am–noon and 1–3pm | stop: San Tomà*

10 SAN SEBASTIANO (124 B4) (*Ш D8*)

The hearts of those who admire the cheerful, opulent paintings of Paolo Veronese will beat faster in this church. What, at first glance, appears to be a

something really special: the works are INSIDER TIP changed several times a day, fully automatically. *Fondamenta Zattere 50 | May–Nov. Wed–Mon 10.30am–6pm | www.fondazionevedova.org | stop: Spirito Santo*

7 PONTE DELL'ACCADEMIA
(125 E4–5) (*Ш F–G 8–9*)

When it was erected in 1932, this wooden bridge was only planned to be a tem-

rather modest church preserves the artistic legacy of this genius. He painted all the paintings on the walls and the high altar and found his final resting place beneath the church's organ. *Mon 10.30am–4pm, Tue–Sat 10.30am–4.30pm | stop: San Basilio*

THE ISLANDS

No exploration of Venice would be complete without visiting at least two or three of the islands off the coast of the *centro storico*.

The view over the lagoon alone makes the trip on the *vaporetto* an unforgettable experience. The small island of Murano is only 15 minutes away by boat and a visit to it and one of its glass-blowing workshops is a classic. On the way, you can stop off at San Michele, the cemetery island. Burano, famous for its lacework, and Sant'Erasmo.

BURANO ● (131 E3) (𝒲 W–X 1–2)
Everything is smaller and more colourful here than in Venice. The island, which is world famous for its embroidered lace *(merletti)*, is a great mood lifter with the brightly coloured façades of the houses. The prettiest one is *Casa di Bepi Suà*, whose unconventional owners have painted it in all sorts of patterns. Then it's onwards over bridges and tiny canals to the *cathedral* of Burano, named after St. Martin. If there's still time after a walk and a drink, then visit the *Museo del Merletto (Tue–Sun 10am–5pm, 6pm in summer). Stop: Burano*

CIMITERO DI SAN MICHELE ★ ●
(123 F1–2) (𝒲 M–N 1–3)
Venice's cemetery island is situated halfway to Murano. Thousands of anony-

mous Venetians have been laid to rest under the cypresses behind the brick walls, as have some prominent visitors from abroad including the composer Igor Stravinsky, the poet Ezra Pound and the great Russian dancer Sergei Diaghilev. *Daily 7.30am–6pm (in winter until 4pm) | stop: Cimitero*

LIDO (131 D–E4) (𝒲 0)
This 12 km/7.5 mi long and 200 m–1.7 km/656 ft–1 mi wide strip of sand protects the city from storms and flooding. Since the 19th century, it has also served the Venetians as a place to spend their leisure time and guests from abroad as a seaside resort. In the early days of tourism, mainly the nobility, the rich and powerful of Europe, as well as privileged artists, enjoyed the dolce far niente on the fine sand of the Lido's beach. The splendid villas, hotels and parks are evidence of this. The loveliest is the Grand Hotel des Bains, built in 1900 and the inspiration behind Thomas Mann's "Death in Venice". Luchino Visconti's fabulous film of this novella takes place here, and "The English Patient" was also filmed at the Des Bains. The end came in 2010. The hotel was closed, and since then has been slowly crumbling away behind a high corrugated steel fence. There were plans for a group of investors to convert it into luxury apartments, and now there is also talk of it re-opening as a hotel, but this could take time. At least the 1930s *Palazzo del Cinema* has been restored and a hall added. Venice's glamorous film festival is held here at the beginning of September.

The aristocratic flair has largely vanished, but the atmosphere and infrastructure for carefree seaside holidays has remained. There are well cared-for beaches with inviting pizzerias, ice cream parlours and bars waiting for sun worshippers and keen swimmers within walking distance of the main road Viale Santa Maria Elisabetta. Night-owls will find several discos, hobby sports enthusiasts rowing and sailing clubs and a network of cycle tracks all over the Lido and the neighbouring island Pellestrina to the south.

It is worth visiting the old Jewish cemetery near the northern tip of the Lido, the INSIDER TIP *Antico Cimitero Ebraico (April–Oct by appointment | tel. 0 41 71 53 59)* and, not far away, the *Aeroporto Nicelli*, an architectural gem in the Bauhaus style.

Those who are interested can take the ferry from Ca' Roman, a small conservation area in the south-west, to the mainland and then travel by bus or – even better – by bike (rental at the Lido *vaporetto* stop, *www.lidoonbike.it*) to Chioggia. But, strictly speaking, this colourful, lively fishing town does not really belong to Venice and is more oriented on the mainland and sea than the lagoon. *Stops: Lido, San Nicolò*

MURANO ★
(131 D3) (*∅ P–S 1–4*)

Comprising five islands and inhabited for around 1400 years, this community (pop. today: almost 7000) is famous for its glass industry. A visit to one of the workshops is an absolute must as is the *Museo del Vetro (daily 10am–6pm, in winter until 5pm | stop: Museo)*. With more than 4000 exhibits, this museum in the Palazzo Giustinian documents the 1000-year history of glass-blowing on Murano. There are even Roman glass objects on display.

The Romanesque former *Santi Maria e Donato Cathedral (Mon–Sat 9am–6pm, Sun 12.30pm–6pm)*, with its two-storey arcades in the choir section and original mosaic floor, as well as the *San Pietro Martire Church (Mon–Fri 9am–5.30pm, Sat/Sun noon–5.30pm)* with one of Giovanni Bellini's major works, will be of particular interest to art lovers. *Various stops*

INSIDER TIP SAN SERVOLO
(131 D4) (*∅ 0*)

This tiny island near the Lido was once the accommodation for the *pazzi clamorosi*, the "dangerous deluded". The psychiatric facility was closed in 1978, and the island was abandoned. Today it is possible to visit the old *manicomio*, the psychiatric ward, and find out more

about the hair-raising treatments used on the mentally ill at the *Museo del Manicomio (mid-May–mid-Sept. Fri 3.30pm–6.30pm, Sat/Sun 11.30am–6.30pm, mid-Sept.–mid-May Mon–Fri 10.45am and 2pm | www.museomanico mio.servizimetropolitani.ve.it)*. Note: Straitjacket and electric shock therapy were only the gentlest methods! *Stop: San Servolo*

SANT'ERASMO (131 E3) (*ŵ O*)

4.4 km/2.7 mi long and 1.2 km/0.75 mi wide: Sant'Erasmo is Venice's kitchen garden. Rare lilac artichokes grow here, as does green, very thin asparagus.

Stroll along the road that circles the island and is virtually without traffic, and through the fields and meadows that are irrigated by narrow canals. Or borrow a bike from *Il Lato Azzurro (Via dei Forti 13 | www.latoazzurro.it)*, a co-operative that also runs a basic hotel and restaurant on the island. Also be sure to visit the INSIDER TIP ▶ *Orto di Venezia* vineyard *(Via delle Motte 1 | ortodivenezia.com)*, which belongs to a strong-minded Frenchman who was the first person to start growing wine here, then take a (swimming) break at the Spiaggia del Bacan at the south-western tip of the island. *Stop: Capannone*

To the south of the Lido, from Malamocco you can see the islet Poveglia

FOOD & DRINK

Many people think that the *cucina veneziana*, with its traditional, exquisite recipes, is still one of the finest cuisines on earth, but there are others who feel that it has been spoiled by mass tourism.

Of course, the admirers and the moaners are both right in a way. There are still many chefs who create wonderful dishes to tickle the diner's palate using the great variety of freshly-caught seafood from the Adriatic and fresh, crisp produce from the "vegetable islands" and mainland, but you will equally find the mass-produced *menu turistico* at a set price – and often, not a very reasonable one at that – served up like a dog's dinner. In any case, the Venetian cuisine still has many incomparable specialities, ranging from the dozens of different varieties of

pasta to the imaginative *frutti di mare* and meat dishes and sweet delights from the cake shops.

Those who want to experience everything the gastronomic landscape of the city has to offer, should start off by going to a few *bacari* (with the stress on the first "a"). These simple stand-up bars are the Venetian equivalent of the Spanish tapas bar, the Parisian bistro or the local pub in Britain – an institution, where you can have a glass of (white) wine, an *ombra*, nibble a couple of delicious snacks, the *cicchetti*, and – first and foremost – have a chat.

Regardless of whether you eat in a gourmet restaurant or trattoria, the classical menu is always the same: you begin with starters *(antipasti)*, followed by

Enjoy the cuisine of the lagoon in countless trattorias, *bacari* and gourmet restaurants in the city

soup, pasta or risotto as the *primo piatto* (first course). The main course *(secondo piatto)* consists of fish or meat with a vegetable or salad side dish *(contorno)*, which must be ordered separately. All of this concludes with a dessert *(dolce)* and/or fruit. This is usually accompanied by wine *(vino)*, often the house wine *(della casa)* with a carafe of water to quench your thirst.

The kitchens are usually open from noon until around 2.30pm for lunch, and from 7pm to around 10pm in the evening. There is almost always an extra cover charge *(pane e coperto)* of 1–3 euros (sometimes more); this includes bread to go with your meal. It will say on the menu if the service charge *(servizio)* is included; if not, a tip of five to ten percent is appropriate – as long as you were satisfied.

BACARI, BARS & OSTERIAS

Locals gather in these generally simply furnished, but extremely cosy wine bars

Sushi and Sashimi in Naranzaria made with fresh fish from the market next door

to have a chat with their neighbours – usually standing up, to eat a few tasty titbits (in the case of the osteria, this is a real meal seated at a table) and knock back an *ombra*, a small glass of white wine that is impossible to imagine Venetian life without.

ACIUGHETA (127 D2–3) (*L7*)

A fine selection of *cicchetti*, pizzas and other delicious things, as well as good wines, just a few yards behind St Mark's Basilica. Soak up the atmosphere at one of the tables outside if the weather is fine. *Daily (sometimes closed Wed in winter) | Campo Santi Filippo e Giacomo 4357 | tel. 0415 22 42 92 | stop: San Zaccaria*

INSIDER TIP DA ALBERTO
(123 D6) (*L5*)

Could it be more Venetian? We think not. Alberto serves typical dishes such as *sarde in saor*, pickled sardines, and bac-

calà mantecato, dried cod cooked in milk and stock until wonderfully creamy, that are just as the Venetians makes them at home. *Daily | Calle Giacinto Gallina 5401 | tel. 0415 23 8153 | www.osteriadaalberto.it | stop: Ospedale*

AMERICAN BAR (126 C3) (*K7*)

Although you can't sit down, the location right below the clock tower on St Mark's Square is unbeatable, the selection of sandwiches and drinks is excellent and the prices – especially compared to the wickedly expensive posh cafés in the area – are pleasantly moderate. Plus, you can still enjoy the unique panorama of the square and the sun at the standing tables outside. *Daily | stop: San Marco*

ANTICO CALICE (126 C1) (*J6*)

Located right around the corner from the lively Campo San Bartolomeo, this storybook Osteria serves up an incredible selection of classic specialities and good wines to a mixed crowd of young locals and tourists in equal measure. *Daily | Calle degli Stagneri 5228 | tel. 04 15 20 97 75 | anticocalice.it | stop: Rialto*

INSIDER TIP OSTERIA BANCOGIRO (122 B6) *(Ø J5–6)*
Hotspot at the fish market near the Rialto Bridge, where the Venetians queue outside the entrance from evening to midnight for cocktails. The kitchen is also excellent. *Closed Mon | Campo San Giacometto 122 | tel. 04 15 23 20 61 | www.osteriabancogiro.it | stop: Rialto*

AL COLOMBO (126 B2) *(Ø J7)*
This establishment serves the same dishes as the gourmet restaurant next door – at half the price. Plus the waiters aren't as stuck up, and everything is a little more down-to-earth – fortunately. *Daily | Corte del Teatro 4619 | tel. 04 15 22 26 27 | www.alcolombo.com | stop: Rialto*

DO MORI ★ (122 B6) *(Ø H5–6)*
Icon – the oldest *bacaro* in Venice. Serving wine (over 100 labels!) and snacks for more than 500 years. The *tramezzini* are delicious. You simply must see it. Unfortunately, because it is now so well-known, it is also overpriced: just close your eyes, and get through it. *Closed Sun and from 8.30pm | Calle dei Do Mori 429 | tel. 04 15 22 54 01 | stop: Rialto*

ENOITECA MASCARETA (127 D1) *(Ø L6)*
The not-quite-successful shabby chic interior and eccentric owner add an entertainment value to the place. The choice of wines is excellent, and as well as serving snacks, you can also get a hearty something for your hunger when it's late. *Closed at lunchtime | Calle Lunga Santa Maria Formosa 5183 |* *tel. 04 15 23 07 44 | www.ostemauroloren zon.com | stop: Ospedale*

AL MERCÀ (122 B6) *(Ø J5)*
A pick-me-up in the open air on a peaceful square near Rialto Bridge: tasty unusual canapés with horsemeat, cauliflower, dried cod or tuna... Good local wine. *Closed Sun | Fondamenta Riva Olio 213 | tel. 0 39 92 47 81 | stop: Rialto*

NARANZARIA ★ (122 B6) *(Ø J5)*
This classy pub in the new trendy quarter between the fish market and Rialto Bridge serves spicy snacks as well as main dishes ranging from carpaccio to couscous, from polenta to pasta, and even sushi, accompanied by excellent wines from Friuli. If the weather is fine, you can sit outside on the Canal Grande until long past midnight. *Nov–March closed Mon | Fondamenta Riva Olio 130 | tel. 04 17 24 10 35 | www.naranzaria.it | stop: Rialto*

★ **Do Mori**
You should treat yourself to a glass of wine in Venice's oldest wine bar → p. 63

★ **Naranzaria**
In this gourmet restaurant, it is possible to sit directly on the Canal Grande until late at night → p. 63

★ **Corte Sconta**
Wonderful fish dishes → p. 66

★ **Gam-Gam**
Now, here's something different: kosher cuisine and Israeli wines in the right place → p. 69

MARCO POLO HIGHLIGHTS

LA RIVISTA (125 E5) (*⟁ F9*)

Stylish wine-and-cheese bar in the cellar of the design hotel Ca' Pisani. Tasty *cicchetti* platter. *Closed Thu | Rio Terà della Mandola 3795 | tel. 04 15 28 37 87 | stop: Sant'Angelo*

Ever tried artichoke ice cream? Or ginger? You'll find the weirdest ice cream flavours in town at the Alaska

cold food and small warm dishes, excellent range of wines; drinks in the Rivista's bar. *Closed Mon | Rio Terrà Foscarini 979 | tel. 04 12 40 14 25 | stops: Accademia, Zattere*

INSIDER TIP ▶ LE SPIGHE ◎
(128 C4) (*⟁ P9*)

Good vegetarian snacks, fresh and organic. To take away or eat at standing tables. Pleasant and cosy. *Mon–Sat 10am–3pm and 5.30–7.30pm | Via Garibaldi 1341 | tel. 04 15 23 81 73 | stop: Arsenale*

TEAMO (126 A2) (*⟁ H7*)

Delicacies in a stylish ambiance – great for a tasty snack or a good chat with a glass of wine or a cocktail. Tip: the mixed *cicchetti* platter. *Closed Thu | Rio Terà della Mandola 3795 | tel. 04 15 28 37 87 | stop: Sant'Angelo*

VECIO FRITOLIN (122 A5) (*⟁ H5*)

Very traditional osteria, full of atmosphere, perfect for a good meal or just a few savoury *cicchetti*. Delicious fish dishes! *Closed Wed lunchtime and Tue | Calle della Regina, 2262 | tel. 04 15 22 28 81 | stop: San Stae*

CAFÉS & ICE CREAM PARLOURS

ALASKA (121 D5) (*⟁ F5*)

This is the most unusual – and probably the smallest – *gelateria* in the city. Carlo Pistacchi makes dozens of exotic and unusual flavours of ice cream from natural ingredients, ranging from asparagus and ginger or artichoke and liquorice to mulberry. Pure bliss! *Daily 11am–11pm;*

in winter noon–10pm, closed Dec/Jan | Calle Larga dei Bari 1159 | stops: Ferrovia, Riva di Biasio

CAFFÈ DEL DOGE (126 B1) (𝄞 J6)

A paradise for caffeine *aficionados* with dozens of coffee varieties. The beans are freshly ground, which smells just wonder-ful. Close to the Rialto Bridge, but slightly hidden down an alley. *Mon–Sat 7am–7pm, Sun (except July/Aug.) 7am–1pm | Calle dei Cinque 609 | stop: San Silvestro, Rialto*

INSIDER TIP ▶ IMAGINA CAFÈ (125 D4) (𝄞 E8)

A great port of call at any time of day

FAVOURITE EATERIES

Captain's Dinner

Oh goodness – ropes on the walls, dark floor boards from the cabins, and in some cases starfish as table decorations – an abundance of clichés. But that's what makes *La Caravella* **(126 A4)** *(𝄞 H8) (daily | Calle Larga XXII Marzo 2399 | tel. 04 15 20 89 01 | www.restaurantlacaravella.com | stop: Giglio | Expensive)* at the Hotel Saturnio & International what it is. The idea – and this is important to the owners – is that you should feel as if you were on an old sailing ship. And the food is simply heavenly! Or do you think you'll find perfectly grilled monkfish, deliciously marinated mussels and perfectly al dente pasta with squid on every street corner in Venice?

Something cheesy going on

Had enough of fish and seafood? The elegant *Da Fiore* **(125 F1)** *(𝄞 G5) (closed Sun/Mon | Calle del Scaleter 2202 | tel. 0 41 72 13 08 | www.dafiore. net | stop: San Stae, San Silvestro | Expensive)* restaurant has a tremendous selection of Italian cheese: fresh, mature, sme... , well, let's just say highly fragrant. So be sure to leave enough room for a cheeseboard – and besides, you'll also have to try the wonderful fruit sorbet at the end, or one of the other popular desserts. Oh, and another thing: there's fish as well.

One for all

You won't be given a menu to choose from here. At the simple *Trattoria dalla Marisa* **(120 C2)** *(𝄞 D2) (closed Mon and Tue evening | Calle delle Canne 652b/Fondamenta San Giobbe | tel. 0 41 72 02 11 | stop: Tre Archi | Budget–Moderate)* there's a set daily menu, and that's it. But what a menu it is: three starters, pasta, main course (meat or fish), dessert – wow! No wonder that the occasional count pops in for lunch as well as labourers and boat skippers. And everyone sits together. The mood may be down-to-earth, but it's honest. A Venetian original.

Dinner for Two

Fabulous 1940s ambience with dark wood, heavy cutlery and fine table linen: the *Ai Gondolieri* **(125 F5)** *(𝄞 G9) (closed Tue | Fondamenta Zorzi 366 | tel. 04 15 28 63 96 | www.aigondolieri.it | stop: Salute | Expensive)* is the kind of place Humphrey Bogart would have taken Ingrid Bergman. The adjoining wine cellar serves excellent wines with a small menu.

or night, for a cappuccino, a quick snack at lunchtime or a cocktail in the evening. Modern design and changing exhibitions by contemporary artists. *Mon–Thu 7am–9pm, Fri/Sat 7am–1pm, Sun 8am–9pm | Rio Terà Canal 3126 | tel. 04 12 41 06 25 | www.imaginacafe.it | stop: Ca' Rezzonico*

TORREFAZIONE CANNAREGIO
(121 E3–4) (*Ω F3*)

Everyone knows the Florian on St. Mark's Square, and this historic coffee house in Cannaregio is just as iconic – with the locals. The prices are normal, and the aroma of the freshly-ground coffee is – wow! *Closed in the evenings | Rio Terà San Leonardo 1337 | www.torrefazionecannar egio.it | stop: Guglie*

RESTAURANTS: EXPENSIVE

ACQUASTANCA (131 D3) (*Ω Q3*)
The two ladies who run this minimalist-modern restaurant really know their

business. Fabulously prepared starters (octopus salad, crispy fried *gamberoni*, creamy dried cod) and the fish dishes are full of flair. Giovanna and Caterina Nason are a great stroke of fortune for the glass-blowing island of Murano. *Closed Sun and evenings except Mon and Fri | Fondamenta Manin 48 | tel. 04 13 19 51 25 | www.acquastanca.it | stop: Murano*

CORTE SCONTA ⭐ (128 A3) (*Ω N8*)
This modestly furnished restaurant is not easy to find but you will be rewarded with an excellent selection of first-class fish. The specials of the day are not listed on the menu but rattled off by the lady of the house in Italian. Trust the chef and order an opulent plate of antipasti. But, be careful: quality has a price! *Closed Sun/Mon | Calle del Pestrin 3886 | tel. 04 15 22 70 24 | www.cortescontavene zia.com | stop: Arsenale*

INSIDER TIP ▶ IL RIDOTTO
(127 D2) (*Ω L7*)

This restaurant, with its brick walls and mirrors and elegant atmosphere, only has enough room for a maximum of 13 guests. Gianni Bonacorsi serves his guests culinary highlights of supreme quality. *Closed Thu at noon and Wed | Campo Santi Filippo e Giacomo 4509 | tel. 04 15 20 82 80 | www.ilridotto.com | stop: San Zaccaria*

RIVIERA (124 C5) (*Ω D9*)
At the western end of the Zattere, the owners Monica and Luca pamper their guests in cosy surroundings, with excellent cooking and fine wines. It is especially delightful eating outside on a sunny day with a view of Giudecca across the wide canal. *Closed Wed/Thu| Fondamenta Zattere al Ponte Lungo 1473 | tel. 04 15 22 76 21 | www.ristoranteriviera.it | stop: San Basilio*

LOW BUDGET

The *Cea* **(123 D5) (*Ω K4–5*)** *(closed Sat evening and Sun | Campiello del Pestrin 5422a | tel. 04 15 23 74 50 | stop: Fondamenta Nuove)* is a simple, friendly trattoria with tables outside and very reasonably-priced risottos, pizzas and fish.

The prices are affordable at the *Caffè Letterario* **(127 D2) (*Ω L6*)** *(Tue–Sun 10am–7pm| Campo Santa Maria Formosa 5252 | tel. 04 12 71 14 11 | stop: San Zaccaria)* on the ground floor of the Fondazione Querini Stampalia, which is a popular meeting place for art students and clerical workers.

RESTAURANTS: MODERATE

ANDRI (131 D4) (*Ø 0*)

Everything is just right here: the freshly prepared food, the reasonable prices, the modern ambience in warm hues, and the warmth and friendliness of the owner Luca. A creative mind. His large-scale pictures hang on the walls, and he also designed the hand-blown wa-

Rosso award. *Closed Tue lunchtime and Mon | Fondamenta della Sensa 3272 | tel. 0 41 72 07 44 | www.osterianicestellato. com | stop: Sant'Alvise*

INSIDER TIP ▶ LINEA D'OMBRA ●
(126 A5) (*Ø H10*)

Creative cooking focussing on sophisticated fish dishes and a list of more than 600 (!) wines draw people to this

Sit right beside the canal in Cannaregio and enjoy the *frutti di mare*: Anice Stellato

ter glasses himself. Come for the second time, and you'll be welcomed like a regular. *Closed Mon/Tue | Via Lepanto 21 | tel. 04 15 26 54 82 | stop: Lido*

OSTERIA ANICE STELLATO
(121 F2) (*Ø G2*)

'In' establishment with yuppie thirty-somethings, and therefore lots of suits and ties. And yet the atmosphere is relaxed and friendly. The fish and seafood dishes have already won a Gambero

smartly designed restaurant. Unforgettable: a meal on the pontoon terrace over the water. *Closed Wed | Zattere/Ponte dell'Umiltà 19 | tel. 04 12 41 18 81 | www. ristorantelineadombra.com | stop: Salute*

OGIO (122 C4) (*Ø K4*)

Hold on, it's going to get kitschy now. What could be better than dinner by candlelight inside ancient monastic ruins? Pop the question here, and she's sure to say yes. Even the food (fish,

LOCAL SPECIALITIES

baccalà mantecato – a paste made of mashed dried cod, garlic, onions and olive oil that is often spread on toast or slices of polenta (photo left)

bigoli in salsa – spaghetti with anchovy sauce

carpaccio – Venice's culinary export hit: wafer-thin slices of raw beef, with a trickle of lemon juice and flakes of Parmesan

cicchetti – Venetian-style tapas: titbits such as small meatballs, tiny fried fish, pickled vegetables, mussels, stuffed olives, slices of polenta, etc. (photo right)

fegato alla venexiana – calf's liver cooked in a white-wine-and-onion stock

fiori di zucca – pumpkin flowers, usually served stuffed and fried

fritto misto di mare – fried fish and seafood

pasta e fagioli – a substantial stew cooked with thick macaroni, white beans and a lot of olive oil

risi e bisi – rice with green peas

risotto nero – creamy, black risotto prepared with squid ink *(seppie)*

sarde in soar – a very traditional, very Venetian, starter: cooked sardines served cold with a marinade of olive oil, vinegar, wine, raisins and pine nuts

tramezzini – triangular white bread sandwiches with cheese, ham, mushrooms, tuna, egg or vegetables and various spreads

meat, vegetarian) is good, but that's actually a minor matter. *Closed Mon evening and Sun | Campo dei Gesuiti 4877 | tel. 0 41 24 11 12 27 | stop: Fondamenta Nove*

INSIDER TIP OSTARIA DA RIOBA
(122 A3) (*H3*)
The best home-made pasta in the city – and of course, fish in every possible variation. Most of the vegetables come from Sant'Erasmo. Creative cuisine, but not too outlandish. *Closed Mon | Fon-*

damenta della Misericordia 2553 | tel. 04 15 24 43 79 | stop: San Marcuola

INSIDER TIP ALLA VECCHIA PESCHERIA ☺ (131 D3) (*Q3*)
An old factory warehouse on Murano decorated with stylish furnishings and contemporary art. Picturesque terrace with a fountain. The menu features creative gourmet dishes made from local organic products farmed on the nearby vegetable islands as well as fish and

dolce alla mamma. Closed Wed | Campiello Pescheria 4 | tel. 04 15 27 49 57 | www.allavecchiapescheria.com | stop: Colonna

VINI DA GIGIO (122 B4) (ᗰ J4)

Seasonal cuisine with lots of Venetian classics. Regulars also appreciate the value for money – so be sure to book in advance. *Closed Mon/Tue | Fondamenta San Felice 3628a | tel. 04 15 28 51 40 | www.vinidagigio.com | stop: Ca' d'Oro*

RESTAURANTS: BUDGET

BANDIERETTE (123 E6) (ᗰ M6)

Good, home-style cooking – something that simple is a rarity in Venice these days. At noon, local workers drop in, whereas in the evening the fare is a bit more up-market. No wonder that it will be hard to find a table if you haven't reserved. *Closed Mon evening and Tue | Barbaria de le Tole 6671 | tel. 04 15 22 06 19 | stop: Ospedale*

CANTINA DO SPADE (122 A6) (ᗰ H5)

Ultra-cosy, tasty, value for money – eat your way down the menu. Typical Venetian cuisine. *Closed Tue lunchtime | Calle delle Spade 860 | tel. 04 15 21 05 83 | www.cantinadospade.com | stop: Rialto*

DUE COLONNE (121 E6) (ᗰ G5)

Those in the know say that this is probably the best pizzeria in town. Venetian *sfiaceti* with ham and horsemeat are also a speciality. *Closed Mon | Campo Sant'Agostin 2343 | tel. 04 17 17 33 8 | stops: San Silvestro, San Stae*

INSIDER TIP ▶ FANTÀSIA ⊘ (127 F3) (ᗰ N8)

The restaurant was opened by an aid organisation that trained young people with disabilities here. They now run the place themselves. The service can sometimes be a little slow, but the pasta, risotti and fish dishes are really good. *Closed Mon | Calle Crosera 3911 | tel. 04 15 22 80 38 | www.ristorantefantasia.it | stop: Arsenale*

GAM-GAM ★ (121 E3) (ᗰ F3)

Kosher cooking in the Jewish-Italian tradition: falafel, gefilte fish and other oriental-style recipes accompanied by excellent Israeli wines. *Closed Fri evening and Sat lunchtime | Sotoportego del Gheto Vecchio 1122 | tel. 04 12 75 92 56 | www.gamgamkosher.com | stop: Guglie*

INSIDER TIP ▶ GHIMEL GARDEN (121 E3) (ᗰ F2)

The most incredible garden and fabulous interior. There are kosher dishes in Jewish cuisine, but there are also vegetarian, vegan and gluten-free ones as well. Shabbat dishes served on Friday evenings and Saturday lunchtimes; book ahead. *Daily | Campo del Ghetto Nuovo | tel. 04 12 43 07 11 | www.ghimelgarden.com | stop: San Marcuola*

OSTERIA AL MERCÀ (131 D–E4) (ᗰ O)

Just a few *cicchetti* with your wine or the full works – the choice is yours. The daily menu costs between 20-25 euros, so you really can't complain. Emphasis on fish. Little wonder – the Osteria is located where the old fish market used to be. Beautifully refurbished, with a conservatory. *Daily | Via Dandolo 17 | tel. 04 12 43 16 63 | www.osteriaalmerca.it | stop: Lido*

INSIDER TIP ▶ TRATTORIA ALLA RAMPA (129 D4) (ᗰ P9)

Hardly any tourists ever come here. But lots of workers and gondolieri do. Large portions, small prices, unfortunately only open at lunchtime. *Closed Sat/Sun and evenings | Via Garibaldi 1135 | tel. 04 15 28 53 65 | stop: Giardini*

SHOPPING

CITY WHERE TO START?
Venice's top boutiques are cheek-by-jowl on the **Mercerie**, the narrow rows of shops between St. Mark's Square and the Rialto Bridge, and along the **Calle Larga XXII Marzo**. Bargain-hunters love browsing through the shops in the alleys to the west of the Rialto Bridge, on the way from there to Campo San Polo and the **Lista di Spagna** near the station, and **Strada Nova** on the hunt for textile and leather goods. The tiny shops in the districts of San Polo and Dorsoduro are full of amusing items, unusual items and genuine handmade items.

Venice is quite an expensive spot. Yet at least leather goods are still cheaper than north of the Alps. The traditional local products make much more interesting souvenirs – lace, hand-printed fabrics, hand-dipped and marbled paper and all other kinds of artistic handwork. Those looking for classical reminders of Venice will not be able to resist taking a carnival mask or vase or bowl of Murano glass back home with them. Culinary specialities, such as cheese or ham, wine, vinegar, oil or special cakes and noodles can also be recommended.

Opening hours are adjusted to the local lifestyle: on working days (including Saturday), the shops usually open their doors some time between 9am and 10am and close at 12.30 or 1pm for a si-

Masks, marbled paper, Murano glass: Venice may not be cheap, but it's an excellent place to find stylish and unusual souvenirs

esta lasting about three hours; they then stay open until 7pm or 7.30pm. Many shops remain closed on Monday morning.

GLASSES

MICROMEGA (126 A4) (*[map] H8*)
Fantastic eyeglasses crafted in-house – chic, simple and ultra-light frames made of gold, titanium or horn. *Calle delle Ostreghe 2436 | www.micromegaottica. com | stop: Giglio*

DELICACIES

ALIANI CASA DEL PARMIGIANO ★
(122 B6) (*[map] J5*)
These people know their cheeses. At Aliani's you get the best Parmesan or exceptional goat's cheese, and everything in excellent packaging that preserves the aroma. Don't miss the big favourite: saffron Pecorino. *Campo Erberia Rialto 214 | www.aliani-casadelparmigiano.it | stop: Rialto Mercato*

MAURO EL FORNER DE CANTON (122 B6) (*[M] H6*)

Biscotti, bruschette, brigiolini, grissini, dolci, pan dei dogi ("doge's bread", a kind of biscuit with hazelnuts)... a great

RIZZO (122 A5) (*[M] H5*)

Oh yes – this shop sells all those wonderful chocolates and biscuits that you'll want to tuck into straight away, beautifully gift-wrapped for you to take along.

You should make sure you're not hungry when you shop at Rizzo

variety of sweet and savoury baked goods. *Ruga Vecchia San Giovanni 603 | www.elfornerdecanton.com | stop: Rialto Mercato*

RIALTO BIOCENTER ♦ (121 F6) (*[M] G–H5*)

Ultra-delicious jams, organic fruit juices, vegan confectionery and macrobiotic pasta sauces – all from certified organic small-scale producers. This is where many locals come for their freshly-baked bread. *Calle della Regina 2264 | stop: Rialto Mercato*

Wine, oil, cheese and cold meats are also sold at its five shops, for instance on the *Calle dei Botteri 1719. www.rizzovenezia.it | stop: Rialto Mercato*

VIZIOVIRTÙ (122 C6) (*[M] K6*)

This chocolate boutique sells all sorts of chocolate, including tiny bars, in traditional and exotic flavours. Be sure to treat yourself to a cup of Goldoni Hot Chocolate – hot chocolate made without milk and sugar. Heavenly! *Calle Forneri 5988 | www.viziovirtu.com | stop: Rialto*

GIFTS & SOUVENIRS

LIBRERIA ACQUA ALTA (127 D1) (*ⓜ L6*)
Pure chaos – this bookshop, with steps made of books, a rear courtyard with wheelbarrows full of them, and a fat cat that spends its time stretched out on art prints, is awesome. Browsing through the mixed offerings until the dust flies – wonderful. Every visit is an experience, whether you want to buy a book or not. *Calle Lunga Santa Maria Formosa 5176 | stop: Ospedale*

ARRAS (125 D3) (*ⓜ F7*)
A large selection of colourful, hand-woven silk, woollen and cotton fabrics. *Campiello Squellini 3235 | stop: Ca' Rezzonico*

INSIDER TIP ► EBRÛ (125 F4) (*ⓜ G8*)
In the 1980s, Alberto Valese was a pioneer of the marbled paper boom, and is still considered one of the masters of this guild today. He stocks the full range: hand-made paper, book covers and a good selection of decorative items. *Campo Santo Stefano 347 | www.albertovalese-ebru.it | stop: San Samuele, Sant'Angelo*

INSIDER TIP ► GILBERTO PENZO (125 E2) (*ⓜ G6*)
Delightful models of Venetian watercraft. You can also buy do-it-yourself gondola model kits; prices start at 25 euros. *Calle Seconda dei Saoneri 2681 | www.veniceboats.com | stop: San Tomà*

MADERA (125 D4) (*ⓜ E8*)
With everything from night-table lamps, tableware, scarves and handbags to unique jewellery, three architects have created a treasure trove of household goods and fashion accessories made of wood, metal and ceramic crafted by young designers. *Campo San Barnaba 2762 and Calle Lunga San Barnaba 2729 | www.maderavenezia.it | stop: Ca' Rezzonico*

SEGRETI DI BELLEZZA (127 E3) (*ⓜ L7*)
Elegant hand-made creams and perfumes with hints of jasmine, amber and saffron. Combined with the flair of the Serenissima: it smells of herbs and spices, as it would have done in the days of the mighty Maritime Republic of Venice, which became rich through trading with the Orient. *Campo San Zaccaria 4695 | www.spezieriadevenezia.com | stop: San Zaccaria*

SIGNOR BLUM ★ (125 D4) (*ⓜ E8*)
Three-dimensional, hand-sawn, unmistakably Venetian, wooden puzzles – a tasteful present! *Campo San Barnaba 2840 | stop: Ca' Rezzonico*

SORELLE SFORZA (125 E2) (*ⓜ F–G6*)
Fabulous smells. individual perfumes, fruity, floral or spicy, and room fragrances made from high-quality natural ingredients. *Calle Seconda dei Saoneri 2658 | stop: San Tomà*

MARCO POLO HIGHLIGHTS

★ **Aliani Casa del Parmigiano**
A dream for all cheese, sausage and ham fans
→ p. 71

★ **Cenedese**
Superlative Murano glass
→ p. 74

★ **Signor Blum**
3-D wooden puzzles as souvenirs → p. 73

Custom work: mask makers

stead of vases and chandeliers, he creates art in glass. All one of a kind – eye-wateringly beautiful, but also eye-wateringly expensive. Be sure to visit the showroom – the wow effect is guaranteed. *Fondamenta Serenella 3 | www. pinosignoretto.it | stop: Murano*

MASKS

The quality manufacturer ● INSIDER TIP▸ Ca' Macana *(www.camacana.com)*, who runs two shops in Dorsoduro (125 D4) *(山 E–F8) (Fondamenta Rezzonico 3172 and Fondamenta Lombardo 1169 | stop: Ca' Rezzonico)*, also offers courses in his studio, where you can be initiated into the art of mask-making either in a group or one-on-one.

Three other mask producers are much more creative than the mass of suppliers: *Tragicomica* (125 E2) *(山 G6) (Calle dei Nomboli 2800 | stop: San Tomà); Mistero Buffo* (124 B4) *(山 D9) (Fondamenta San Basilio 1645 | stop: San Basilio); Marega* (127 E2) *(山 L7) (Fondamenta dell'Osmarin 4968 and 4976a | stop: San Zaccaria)*

GLASS

CENEDESE ★ (131 D3) *(山 Q4)*
For brightly-coloured, modern chandeliers. And these plain, slender vases called Vela will go with any interior – it's worth the investment. *Fondamenta Vetrai 68 | www.simonecenedese.it | stop: Murano*

GAMBARO & POGGI (131 D3) *(山 Q2)*
For more than a quarter of a century, Mario Gambaro and Bruno Poggi have given full rein to their creativity: vases, jugs, glasses, chandeliers... 1300 articles in 85 colours that you can admire, and buy, here. *Calle del Cimitero 15 | www. gambaroepoggiglass.com | stop: Venier*

PINO SIGNORETTO (131 D3) *(山 P4)*
The superstar of the glass-blowers. In-

FASHION

INSIDER TIP▸ ACQUA MAREA ◎ (125 D2) *(山 E7)*
Wellies, wellies and more wellies – tremendous selection and good prices. Let the floods come. Also sells vegan shoes made of canvas and other natural materials. *Campo San Pantalon 3750 | stop: San Tomà*

GIULIANA LONGO (126 B1) *(山 J6)*
Hats in the style of the gondolieri or fancy hats for carnival – in this wonderfully old-fashioned hat shop, even trying on the various models is great fun. Every single hat is hand-made, and Giuliana will

find the right one for any head. *Calle del Lovo 4813 | www.giulianalongo.com | stop: Rialto*

INSIDER TIP ▶ MALEFATTE ✪
(125 F4) (*ω G8*)

Shopping and social assistance all rolled into one. High-quality organic cosmetics, notepads, t-shirts and original bags made by the inmates of the municipal prison are sold by a cooperative at a kiosk on Campo Santo Stefano (or on-line: *www.malefatte.org*). *Mon, Tue, Thu 10am–3pm | stop: San Samuele*

PENNY LANE ✪ (124 C2) (*ω E6*)

This shop will have vintage-lovers gasping for breath. All sort of ordinary and off-the-wall items, organic and FairTrade labels, handbags and accessories made from recycled materials. *Salizada San Pantalon 39 | stop: San Tomà*

JEWELLERY

LABERINTHO (125 F1) (*ω G5*)

Several young goldsmiths have joined forces here to present their imaginative creations. *Calle del Scaletter 2236 | laberintho.it | stop: San Silvestro*

MANUELA ZANVETTORI
(131 D3) (*ω Q4*)

This woman knows what women want: necklaces, earrings and bracelets made of glass, gold and silver. She grew up in a family of glass-blowers. So it's understandable that it should be her favourite material. *Fondamenta dei Vetrai 122 | www.manuela zanvettori.com | stop: Murano*

SHOES & LEATHER GOODS

BALDUCCI (121 E4) (*ω F3*)

The softest, smoothest leather from Tuscany, and worked to Venetian tradition. It started in 1974 with bags, and today it also stocks hand-stitched shoes and belts. *Very classic*, but also perfect for an elegant appearance. *Rio Terà San Leonardo 1593 | www.balducciborse.com | stop: Guglie, San Marcuola*

FRATELLI ROSSETTI (126 B3) (*ω J8*)

A treasure chest for all lovers of fashionable footwear. *Salizada San Moisè 1477 | stop: Vallaresso*

INSIDER TIPP ▶ PIEDÀTERRE
(122 B6) (*ω J6*)

The soft-as-silk slippers *(furlane)* with their non-slip rubber soles that the gondolieri wear when they are working used to be available in many shops. Today, cheap reproductions from the Far East have flooded the market. But here you will still find the original – of linen, with or without silk ribbons in all kinds of bright colours. Price from 32 euros for a pair. *Ruga degli Oresi 60 | stop: Rialto Mercato*

LOW BUDGET

Fish, fruit, vegetables and spices are cheapest at the small markets, e.g. *Campo Santa Margherita* **(125 D3)** *(ω E7)* or *Rio Terà San Leonardo* **(121 E4)** *(ω G3) (both Mon–Sat 8am–2pm)* than in shops.

Chic, reasonably-priced dresses, jackets, bags and many more articles made of silk, velvet and brocade, tailored by the female inmates of the Giudecca Prison, are available at ✪ *Banco No. 10* **(127 F2–3)** *(ω M7) (Salizada Sant'Antonin 3478a | stop: San Zaccaria)*. Each piece is unique.

ENTERTAINMENT

CITY **WHERE TO START?**

The liveliest places are the **Campi Santa Margherita** area and **San Pantalon**, and along the wide **canals of Cannaregio**. There are rows and rows of bars, pubs and artists' cafés, some with live performances. The Venetians also like to meet up on the **Campi San Bartolomeo** or **San Lio**. For hot summer nights: the ● **open-air establishments on the Canal Grande** next to the Fabbriche Vecchie.

Yes, Venice has a night-life. Unfortunately, it's something that most day-trippers miss – but it's worth experiencing it.

Some clubs rock until the small hours, and for those who want something really special, the La Fenice opera house is the place to go. Of course, the very best time to go is during the carnival, with its semi-public parties and smart costumed balls (don't even ask how much it costs to get in; just accept that it's worth the money).

Between March and October, you'll be spoilt for choice every evening, with everything from jazz to chamber concerts, and plenty in between. And there's plenty of singing and music in churches, monasteries and fraternities all over the city. If you can speak Italian, you will enjoy exploring the theatre and cabaret world. Some of the productions are on an international level; La Fenice in particular is well-

A lively bar and pub scene: nightlife pulsates on the streets and squares of Venice

known for its lavish performances with all-star casts. If you want to spend lots of money, the best place to go is the the famous casino, to spend an evening feeling like Daniel Craig as James Bond in Casino Royale. But there are less expensive ways to pass the time: grab a beer or a glass of wine, and join the bustling throngs than create an incomparable atmosphere until well after midnight on the *Campi Santa Maria Formosa, Santa Margherita, Pisani, San Barnaba* and *Santi Giovanni e Paolo.* Street art and spontaneous gigs are not rare in summer, and the cicchetti in the bars are really delicious. For current information, ask your hotel for the free calendar of events published by the tourist office, or have a look at *www.aguestin venice.com, www.venezianews.it, www. meetingvenice.it.*

BARS, PUBS, CLUBS, CAFÉS & LIVE MUSIC

ART BLU CAFFÈ (125 F4) *(⑪ G8)*
A bright and friendly eatery with a func-

tional modern look. Best tip: the ☽ terrace with its amazing panorama – ideal for a nightcap at the end of the day. *Daily until 11pm | Campo Santo Stefano 2808a | stop: San Samuele*

BACARO JAZZ (122 C6) (*罒 J6*)
Well-stocked cocktail bar serving food (until 2am!) with a unique and colourful

Musicians like Sting and Hollywood stars on the level of Al Pacino or Daniel Craig often pop in for a drink. *Campo San Moisè 1459 | tel. 04 15 20 70 22 | www.bbarvenezia.com | stop: Vallaresso*

CAFÉ NOIR (125 D2) (*罒 E–F7*)
Quirky but charming bar with a stylish interior and unusually great prices. Popu-

The Centrale is bar, lounge and restaurant all rolled into one

ambiance. An ideal place for jazz lovers and night owls. *Daily 11am–ca.2.30am, Happy Hour 4pm–6pm | Salizada del Fondaco dei Tedeschi 5546 | stop: Rialto*

B-BAR ● (126 B4) (*罒 J8*)
Fancy some celebrity-watching? The VIP presence in the lounge of the luxury hotel Bauer is traditionally high. So order yourself a cocktail (they really are extremely good!) and relax in an armchair.

lar among students and the Happy Hour *aperitivi* are very inexpensive. *Mon–Sat 7am–2am, Sun 9am–2am | Crosera San Pantalon 3805 | stop: San Tomà*

CAFFÈ ROSSO (125 D3) (*罒 E7*)
In a lovely spot that is bustling until after midnight. An absolute hotspot of the open-air night-life, with live music in summer and – comparatively – low prices. Be sure to try the delicious *tramezzini!*

Mon–Sat 7am–1am | Campo Santa Margherita 2963 | stop: Ca' Rezzonico

CENTRALE (126 B3) (*Ø J8*)

Trendy, international class, restaurant-bar. The food is well above average and the atmosphere stylish. But rather pricey. *Sun–Thu 7pm–midnight, Fri/Sat 7pm–1am | Piscina Frezzeria 1659 | www.caffe centralevenezia.com | stop: Vallaresso*

MARGARET DUCHAMP
(125 D3) (*Ø E7*)

'In' bar with lovely barkeepers. The cocktails are among the best in the city, and the Campo is active until late at night. Open until 2am! *Closed Tue | Campo Santa Margherita 3019 | stop: Ca' Rezzonico*

UN MONDO DI VINO (122 C5) (*Ø K5*)

Tiny pub with delicious *cicchetti* and not much room. A glass of wine costs between 1.50 and 3 euros – just what you need to warm up. The later the hour, the longer the queue outside the door. *Daily from 10am–11.30pm | Salizada San Canciano 5984 | www.unmondodivinove zia.com | stop: Ca' d'Oro*

INSIDER TIP ▶ IL SANTO BEVITORE
(122 A3–4) (*Ø H3*)

Twenty types of draught beer for those who are getting a little tired of wine and spritzers. Always a pleasant atmosphere. *Daily from 4pm–2am | Campo Santa Fosca 2393a | www.ilsantobevitorepub.com | stop: San Marcuola*

SENSO UNICO/CORNER PUB
(125 F5) (*Ø G9*)

And now for something completely different: Small Britain in Venice. Naturally beer is drunk here rather than wine – and a rather good one at that. Lots of students from the UK come here to drown their homesickness. *Wed–Mon*

10.30am–1am | Calle della Chiesa 684 | stop: Accademia

TORINO@NOTTE (126 B2) (*Ø J7*)

Only three minutes from Piazza San Marco: long drinks, snacks and hot music; live jam-sessions on Wed. *Tue–Sat 7pm–1am, bar open from 8am | Campo San Luca 459 | stop: Rialto*

INSIDER TIP ▶ VENICE JAZZ CLUB
(125 D4) (*Ø E8*)

A little bit like a living room party. Guests sit together with finger food and relaxed music, then there's some jazz (the in-house band is the VJC Quartet), and by the end of the evening they're all the best of friends. *Happy Hour from 7pm, concert starts at 9pm Mon–Wed, Fri, Sat 7pm–1am | Ponte dei Pugni 3102 | www. venicejazzclub.com | stop: Ca' Rezzonico*

DISCOTHEQUES & BEACH PARTIES

In summer, people head to the Lido to party. Travel out on the night *vaporetto* (line N) from San Zaccaria. Get off, and head straight for the beach! In the evenings, the lidos become lounge bars with DJ sets, such as the *Pachuka (daily from 9am–10pm, longer at weekends | Viale Klinger/Spiaggia San Nicolò)*. Fish restaurant, pizzeria and cocktail bar in one: the *Terrace Beach (Lungomare Guglielmo Marconi 22)*. Or do like the young Venetians do, and stock up on snacks and drinks at one of the beach kiosks, then find yourself a pleasant spot – for instance at the *Chiosco Bahiano* on the northern end of the beach on the *Piazza Pola*.

There are no big discos in the old town; there simply isn't the space, and noise pollution is also an issue. But on the plus side, at the *Piccolo Mondo* (125 E5) (⌕ F9) *(daily from 11pm–4am | Calle Contarini Corfù 1056a | stop: Accademia)* you can dance until 4am. Lots of international artists tend to pop in late at night, as well as Venetians. Even Mick Jagger has been spotted here ...

CASINO

● Today, you can try your luck behind the impressive façade of the *Palazzo Vendramin-Calergi* (121 F4) (⌕ G4) on the Canal Grande where Richard Wagner wrote "Parsifal". Roulette, blackjack, gaming machines, etc. *Daily 3.30pm–2.45am | www.casinovenezia.it | stop: San Marcuola*

CINEMA

Most of the films shown in the few remaining cinemas in Venice have been synchronised into Italian but there is one exception:

INSIDER TIP CASA DEL CINEMA
(121 F5) (⌕ G5)

This meeting place for cineastes next to the Palazzo Mocenigo shows high-quality films from all over the world, partly in the original version with Italian subtitles. *Salizada San Stae 1990 | tel. 04 15 24 13 20 | stop: San Stae*

CONCERTS

COLLEGIUM DUCALE

If you're going for classical, then get it right. The chamber orchestra was founded in 1993, and performs wonderful instrumental works from the Baroque and Romantic periods, but also performs with opera singers the favourite arias from Carmen, Otello and other operas accompanied by a piano. The venues are just as impressive: the *Palazzo delle Prigioni* (127 D3) (⌕ L8) and the "Blue Room" of the *Teatro San Gallo* (126 B3) (⌕ J7). *Tel. 0 41 98 81 55 | www.collegiumducale.com*

INTERPRETI VENEZIANI ★ ●
(125 F4) (⌕ G8)

This chamber music group gives concerts entitled "Violins in Venice" on more than 200 days of the year in the former San Vidal Church. The highlights of the programme include works by Bach, Vivaldi, Tartini & Co. *Tel. 0412 7705 61 | www.interpretiveneziani.com*

VIRTUOSI DI VENEZIA
(126 C2–3) (*∭ K7*)

Baroque orchestral music hits, ranging from Vivaldi's "Four Seasons" to Albinoni's Adagio – as well as arias by Mozart, Verdi and Donizetti. Dressed in period costume, the Virtuosi di Venezia give several concerts of opera and orchestral classics weekly in the Ateneo di San Basso behind St Mark's Basilica. *Piazzetta dei Leoni | tel. 0415 28 28 25 | www.virtuosidivenezia.com*

SHOW

VENEZIA – THE SHOW (126 B3) (*∭ J7*)
An elaborate multi-media spectacle: actors in historical costumes talk (in English, simultaneous translation through headphones) about Venice's more than 1000 years of history supported by cutting-edge digital technology; the show can also be booked together with a buffet dinner. *Campo San Gallo 1097 | tel. 0412 41 20 02 | www.teatrosangallo.net*

THEATRE & OPERA

TEATRO LA FENICE ⭐
(126 A3) (*∭ H8*)

The theatre burned to the ground in 1996 but the old "Phoenix" rose again from the ashes and was reopened in 2003 – "dov'era e com'era" where and as it was – on Campo Fantin in the form of a time-honoured, golden shimmering theatre with rows of boxes. In Venice, tickets for the excellently cast opera and dance performances (the Fenice is one of the leading opera houses of Europe), as well as concerts, are available from the theatre's box office and the Ve.La. tick-

A temple of the muses since 1678: Teatro Malibran

et offices at the railway station and Piazzale Roma. Information and tickets from abroad: *tel. 0 41 24 24. Campo San Fantin 1965 | www.teatrolafenice.it | stop: Giglio*

TEATRO MALIBRAN (122 C6) (*∭ K5–6*)
Opera, ballet, concerts and plays; some in cooperation with the Teatro Fenice. *Programme information and tickets at Campiello del Teatro | 5864 tel. 0 41 24 24 | www.teatrolafenice.it | stop: Rialto*

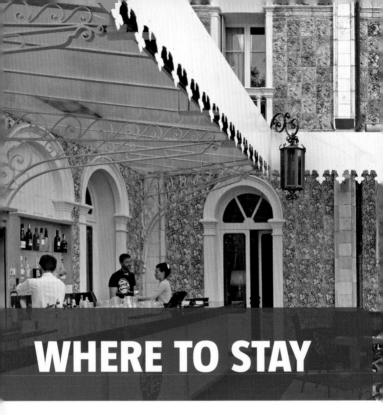

WHERE TO STAY

There are plenty of hotels in Venice – in every part of the city and every price category. But instead of heading to the nearest reception desk, compare prices first. Value for money is often appalling – although it can vary tremendously from season to season.

If money is no object, then head straight for one of the top hotels that are so popular with Hollywood stars and industrial magnates. Standing next to Angelina Jolie at the breakfast buffet – now there's an idea. Even if you go for one star less, the atmosphere is still sure to be exclusive. And the price for a night still horrendous. But the cheaper the establishment, the more care you need to take. Photos of sparsely furnished "closets" are usually shot with wide-angle lenses, and most likely to be cells rather than rooms.

In peak season, a pleasant double room in a central location – that is, from Easter until the end of October, at Christmas/ New Year and carnival – can easily set you back 200 euros. If you want cheap accommodation, it's a good idea to close you eyes when you enter you room – or come in winter. There aren't so many tourists around then, and hotel rooms can be between 30 and 50 percent cheaper. Another rule of thumb if you want to save money is the further you are from St. Mark's Square, the better the prices. Whenever you come, there is also a tourist charge per guest and night that, depending on the hotel category, is between 1 and 8 euros (half that during the low season).

Whether on the Canal Grande, in the midst of the labyrinth of small streets, or with a view of a beach on the Adriatic: the best places to stay

It's better if you book in advance, as otherwise the hotels and guesthouses that offer the best value of the 400 or so in the city will already be full. Not surprising, really, when you consider that the city has 4 million overnight guests a year. As well as the usual hotel portals, the following websites also offer a good selection of accommodation: *www.venice hotel.com, www.cross-pollinate.com.* An apartment is a good alternative for families and groups in particular. In addition to being available for a whole week, you can also book them by the day – and you'll have cooking facilities as well.

A word about prices: our classification – see page 4 – is based on the average price for the season in the most inexpensive double room in the hotel or guesthouse. As demand often exceeds supply, and there is hardly a genuine "off-season" in Venice, you should expect on prices considerably above those quoted. On the other hand, the global economic crisis has had a severe impact on Venice and an increasing number of hoteliers

Fabulous lamps and vintage furniture: Philippe Starck had the time of his life working on the Palazzina G project

have been forced to lower their prices – a phenomenon that not only, but mainly, applies to the more expensive hotels, which often grant substantial discounts now if the hotel is not fully booked. In any case, you should check the webiste of individual hotels and international sites for the latest special offers. And if you telephone or book when you arrive, always ask for *sconto,* especially if you are staying for several nights.

HOTELS: EXPENSIVE

GRANDE ALBERGO AUSONIA & HUNGARIA (131 D–E4) (*Ø 0*)

A hotel gem lies hidden behind the fairy-tale art nouveau façade of majolica tiles on the main street on the Lido halfway between the lagoon and the Adriatic. Most of the furniture is still original art nouveau; there is an elegant dining room with a bar, a winter veranda and terrace. Includes the Thai spa *Lanna Gaia. 88 rooms | Gran Viale Santa Maria Elisabetta 28 | tel. 0412420060 | www. hungaria.it | stop: Lido*

CONCORDIA ★ ☆ (126 C2–3) (*Ø K7*)

As central as it gets: the only hotel with a view of St Mark's Basilica and Square has a slightly chilly charm, but the service and comfort are first-rate. The breakfast buffet facing the Campanile is unforgettable. *56 rooms | Calle Larga San Marco 367 | tel. 0415206866 | www.hotel concordia.it | stop: San Marco*

METROPOLE ● (127 E3) (*Ø M8*)

Opulent, Baroque interior with gold-plated chandeliers, grandfather clocks and mirrors. Excellent restaurant. Don't forget to ask for a room with a view of the lagoon! *67 rooms | Riva degli Schiavoni 4149 | tel. 04 15 20 50 44 | www.hotel metropole.com | stop: San Zaccaria*

PALAZZINA G (125 E3) (*ⓤ F7–8*)

The famous French designer Philippe Starck has turned this small building next to the museum Palazzo Grassi into a contemporary boutique hotel worthy of its five stars. With much attention to detail, the lobby, lounge, and restaurant/bar have been outfitted with a mix of vintage furniture and lush colours, but the 26 rooms have been kept all in white. *Ramo Grassi 3247 | tel. 04 15 28 46 44 | www. palazzinag.it | stop: San Samuele*

RUZZINI PALACE ★ (127 D1) (*ⓤ K6*)

Elegant and pleasant – can you have both? Yes, you can! This 4-star hotel has class and only a few rooms, which means guests aren't treated as if on a conveyor belt, but always receive a friendly welcome. The location is unbeatable: it's on one of the prettiest squares in Venice, and yet not in the middle of all the hustle and bustle. *11 rooms | Campo Santa Maria Formosa 5866 | tel. 04 12 41 04 47 | www. ruzzinipalace.com | stop: San Zaccaria*

SATURNIA & INTERNATIONAL
(126 A4) (*ⓤ H8*)

A hotel palace from the 14th century. Most of the agreeably spacious rooms face the inner courtyard and ooze quality. *89 rooms | Calle Larga XXII Marzo 2398 | tel. 04 15 20 83 77 | www.hotelsat urnia.it | stop: Giglio*

HOTELS: MODERATE

AGLI ALBORETTI (125 E5) (*ⓤ F9*)

OK, the rooms may be small, but they have everything you need and are comfortable. Breakfast is served in the pretty courtyard. *23 rooms | Rio Terà Foscarini 884 | tel. 04 15 23 00 58 | www. aglialboretti.com | stop: Accademia*

BECHER (126 B3) (*ⓤ H7–8*)

A still rather new, very pleasant three-star hotel near Teatro Fenice. Breakfast in your room at no extra charge. Half of the rooms have a view of the canal. *17 rooms | Calle del Fruttarol 1857 | tel. 04 15 22 12 53 | www.hotelbecher.com | stop: Vallaresso*

CASA REZZONICO ★ (125 D4) (*ⓤ E8*)

Informal hotel only two minutes from the trendy Campo Santa Margherita district. Breakfast is served in the tranquil garden. *14 rooms | Fondamenta Gheradini 2813 | tel. 04 12 77 06 53 | www.casarez zonico.it | stop: Ca' Rezzonico*

GABRIELLI ☽ (127 F3) (*ⓤ N8*)

This Gothic-style building is full of atmosphere, has large rooms, an idyllic green

---

★ Concordia
The perfect place to stay with a view of Saint Mark's Square
→ p. 84

★ Ruzzini Palace
It took ten years to convert this elegant palazzo, and it is now a small, exclusive deluxe hotel
→ p. 85

★ Generator Hostel Venice
Youth hostel with a great view
→ p. 88

★ Casa Rezzonico
Stay at the heart of the Campo Santa Margherita, breakfast in the quiet garden → p. 85

MARCO POLO HIGHLIGHTS

courtyard and the view from the roof terrace is a dream. Don't forget to book a room looking towards the lagoon! *103 rooms | Riva degli Schiavoni 4110 | tel. 04 15 23 15 83 | www.hotelgabrieli.it | stop: Arsenale*

LOCANDA DEL GHETTO (121 E3) (*M F2*)
Stay in the heart of the former Jewish Ghetto in a six-hundred-year-old building one floor below the former synagogue. Well looked-after, good breakfast and pleasant service. The two junior suites have INSIDER TIP charming terraces overlooking the central square. *6 rooms | Campo del Ghetto Novo 2892 | tel. 04 12 75 92 92 | www.locandadelgheto. net | stop: Guglie*

OLTRE IL GIARDINO (125 E1) (*M F6*)
You'll instantly feel at home here. The rooms are charming, and the garden is enchanting. In the 1920s, the house belonged to the eccentric Alma Mahler, wife of the composer. *6 rooms | Fondamenta Contarini 2542 | tel. 04 12 75 00 15 | www.ol treilgiardino-venezia.com | stop: San Tomà*

INSIDER TIP ► **AL PONTE MOCENIGO** (121 F5) (*M G4*)
Tastefully styled standard hotel, pleasantly low-priced. Breakfast and drinks in the shady courtyard. All rooms with bathroom and air-conditioning. *10 rooms | Fondamenta Rimpetto Mocenigo 2063 | tel. 04 15 24 47 97 | www.alpontemoceni go.com | stop: San Stae*

MORE THAN A GOOD NIGHT'S SLEEP

Art déco and Co.
The Ca' Pisani Hotel **(125 E5)** (*M F9*) *(29 rooms | Calle Larga Pisani 979a | tel. 04 12 40 14 11 | www.capisanihotel.it | stop: Accademia | Expensive)* was the city's first designer hotel, and is still its best. A Venetian palazzo dating back to the 14th century – with furniture from the 1930s and 40s in the rooms. Originals by the Italian Futurists on the walls. Every detail is absolutely perfect here, so please remember to bring a suit and heels!

Relax with views
Would you like to enjoy the panoramic views of the Giudecca Canal and St. Mark's Square while you wait for your spa treatment? You can at the ● ☆ Palladio Hotel & Spa **(131 D4)** (*M K11*) *(79 rooms | Fondamenta Zitelle 33 | tel. 04 15 20 70 22 | www.palladiohotelspa. com | stop: Zitelle | Expensive)*, an ultra-

deluxe 5-star establishment within the walls of an old monastery with wonderful hidden gardens. On sunny days, you can enjoy a massage amongst the trees and flowers, well out of sight of curious passers-by. In bygone days, this was a home for unmarried girls from good families. Which makes it just the place for a girls' weekend!

Crazy on the island
Small budget = small room? *Nooooo!* At the Centro Soggiorno e Studi San Servolo **(131 D4)** (*M 0*) *(173 rooms | tel. 04 12 76 50 01 | short.travel/ven1 | stop: San Servolo | Budget)* on the tiny island of the same name, the rooms are large and inexpensive. Like the rest of the estate, a former psychiatric facility for the dangerously demented (– but then, don't we all sometimes have our moments?).

SAN GALLO (126 B3) (*M J7*)
Small, charming hotel on a campo that is just as lovely only a few yards north of Piazza San Marco with a breakfast terrace on the roof. *12 rooms | Campo San Gallo 1093a | tel. 04 15 22 73 11 | www.hotelsan gallo.com | stops: Rialto, Vallaresso*

VILLA MABAPA ꙮ (131 E4) (*M 0*)
Smart hotel in a villa at the northern corner of the Lido that is hardly affected by tourism. Lovely view of the old city and a restaurant with garden terrace. *60 rooms | Riviera San Nicolò 16 | tel. 04 15 26 05 90 | www.villamabapa.com | stop: Lido*

HOTELS: BUDGET

LOCANDA AI BARETERI (126 C2) (*M J7*)
Quiet yet central location. It's only a jump to the lively Rialto quarter for a cocktail. The lovely owners even collect their guests from the *vaporetto* station. No elevator, and not all rooms have their own bathroom. *12 rooms | Calle di Mezzo 4966 | tel. 04 15 23 22 33 | www. bareteri.it | stop: Rialto*

CA' DEL DOSE (127 F3) (*M M8*)
Guesthouse in a small side street at the eastern end of the Riva degli Schiavoni. Contemporary ambience in warm colours, very functional interiors. Also offers three holiday apartments. *6 rooms | Calle del Dose 3801 | tel. 04 15 20 98 87 | www. cadeldose.com | stop: Arsenale*

CAPRERA (121 D4) (*M E4*)
If you can do without an en-suite bathroom, this is a cheap place to stay near the railway station. Some of the renovated rooms have a small balcony – it's worth asking for one! *14 rooms | Lista di Spagna 219 | tel. 0 41 71 52 71 | www.hotel caprera.it | stop: Ferrovia*

DOMUS CILIOTA (125 F4) (*M G8*)
Once an abbey guesthouse, now privately run. Still spartan, but bright, clean and inexpensive, and friendly hosts. The fabulous location near the Campo Santo Stefano eliminates the need for lots of *vaporetto* rides. *50 rooms | Calle delle Muneghe 2976 | tel. 04 15 20 48 88 | www.ciliota.it | stop: San Samuele*

DONI (127 D–E3) (*M L7–8*)
This pleasant guesthouse with wooden floors is a place where you will feel at home. The only drawback: nine of the 13 rooms have their bathroom on the landing. *Calle del Vin 4656 | tel. 04 15 22 42 67 | www.albergodoni.it | stop: San Zaccaria*

AI DUE FANALI (121 D5) (*M E4*)
Quiet, impeccable hotel, with reasonable prices, only a few yards from the railway station. An interesting alternative for groups: the owner also has four suites, each of 50m^2 and with three beds on the Riva degli Schiavoni. Main building: *16 rooms | Campo San Simeon Grande 946 | tel. 0 41 71 84 90 | www.aiduefanali. com | stop: Ferrovia*

INSIDER TIP ▶ **FORESTERIA LEVI** (125 E4) (*M G8*)
A lovely guesthouse at affordable prices – and that in the middle of San Marco. You can even walk through the courtyard directly to the Canal Grande. The palazzo is the home of the Ugo and Olga Levi Foundation, which organises concerts and cultural events here.
If you are interested in classical music, the Foundation's own library on the musical history of Venice is practically outside your room. *20 rooms | Calle Vitturi o Falier 2893 | tel. 0 41 78 67 77 | www.fores terialevi.it | stop: Accademia*

GUERRATO (122 B6) (Ⓜ *J5*)
This small, simple, but well cared-for albergo is located in an 800-year-old building and has, by Venetian standards, comparatively large, bright rooms, some of them with a picturesque view of the vegetable market. *20 rooms | Calle dietro la Scimmia 240a | tel. 04 15 28 59 27 | www. pensioneguerrato.it | stop: Rialto*

PAGANELLI (127 E3) (Ⓜ *L8*)
Breathtaking views of the lagoon from

LOW BUDGET

This establishment used to be the city youth hostel, and was housed in the former grain store on Giudecca Island. Today the rooms are modern and available to all ages, still at extremely reasonable prices. The location right on the promenade with mooring is ultra-practical, while the picture-book views of the Doge's Palace and Campanile are breathtaking. It is essential to book in advance. The price for a night's accommodation in a multiple room with breakfast is from 30 euros, depending on the season. ★ ☆ *Generator Hostel Venice* **(131 D4)** (Ⓜ *J11*) *(27 rooms with 235 beds | Fondamenta delle Zitelle 86 | tel. 04 18 77 82 88 | www.gener atorhostels.com | stop: Zitelle*

Another alternative to the hotels in Venice is the *Campeggio San Nicolò* **(131 E4)** (Ⓜ *0*) *(Via di Sammicheli 14 | tel. 04 15 26 74 15 | www.camp ingsannicolo.com)*: this is a well-run camp site with space for 174 tents on the north tip of the Lido.

the ☆ rooms on the south side of this hotel. The other building on nearby Campo San Zaccaria is just as good. *22 rooms | Riva degli Schiavoni 4687 | tel. 04 15 22 43 24 | www.hotelpaganelli. com | stop: San Zaccaria*

SANT'ANNA (129 D4) (Ⓜ *Q8*)
Well-maintained, very pleasant one-star accommodation in a quiet location at the edge of the old city centre just a three minutes' walk from the Biennale grounds. Terrace solarium, relaxed atmosphere, rooms with bath (from 50 euros) and without (from 45 euros). *8 rooms | Corte del Bianco 269 | tel. 04 15 28 64 66 | www.locandasantanna. com | stop: Giardini*

INSIDER TIP ▶ **VENICE CERTOSA HOTEL** (131 D–E 3-4) (Ⓜ *0*)
This place is not only an alternative to normal hotels in the Old City for water sports' enthusiasts: the small, very personally-run hotel is attached to the extremely modern yachting centre that has been established on the island of the same name. Smart, functional, decorated in cheerful colours and with spacious gardens, but only a few minutes by *vaporetto* from the centro storico, it is a real oasis of tranquillity. ◉ You can rent canoes and boats to explore the lagoon at your own pace. *25 rooms | Certosa Island | tel. 04 12 77 86 32 | www.ventodi venezia.com | stop: Certosa*

INSIDER TIP ▶ **OSTELLO VENISSA** ◉ (131 E3) (Ⓜ *V1*)
A taste of rural Venice for connoisseurs on the little island of Mazzorbo next to Burano. This country estate with extensive gardens features an organic gourmet restaurant as well as a small hotel in the main house with 6 airy and charming rooms decorated with a mix of contemporary

Stylish youth hostel with a fabulous, panoramic view

and country-style furnishings. Double rooms from 100 euros. *Fondamenta Santa Caterina 3 | tel. 0415272281 | www.venissa.it | stop: Mazzorbo*

APARTMENTS

As an alternative to hotels and guesthouses, there are numerous fully furnished apartments and holiday homes that can usually be booked for a minimum of three days. You'll find a large selection at a range of prices (some also B&B) at: *www.welcomevenice.com (tel. 0415225251)*, *www.appartamentivenezia.it (tel. 33 46 04 58 50)*, *www.veniceapartment.com*, *www.viewsonvenice.com (tel. 0412411149)* and *www.cabadoerveniceflat.it.*

INSIDER TIP ▶ **ALLOGGI TEMPORANEI**
(125 E4) (*ull* G8)

This agency has around 100 different places to stay, ranging from single rooms in private homes to spacious flats. *Calle Vitturi o Faller 2923 | tel. 0415231672 | www.mwz-online.com | stop: San Samuele*

CA' DELLA CORTE

The people who run this average-standard hotel ((124 C2) (*ull* E6) *Corte Surian 3560*) also have four elegant flats to rent. Very comfortable and fully equipped, suitable for families with small children, luggage transfer, laundry service – and even breakfast can be provided. *Tel. 041715877 | www.cadellacorte.com | stop: Piazzale Roma*

DISCOVERY TOURS

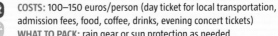

① VENICE AT A GLANCE

START: ① Santa Lucia train station
END: ⑮ Art Blu Caffè

Distance:
➡ ca. 12 km/7.5 mi

1 day
Walking time
(without stops)
approx. 3 1/2 hours

COSTS: 100–150 euros/person (day ticket for local transportation, admission fees, food, coffee, drinks, evening concert tickets)
WHAT TO PACK: rain gear or sun protection as needed

IMPORTANT TIPS: you can vary the starting point of this tour depending on the location of your hotel – just start from the closest vaporetti stop to your neighbourhood. You can only tour the Cathedral and climb the Campanile at the times provided during the main season between Easter and October because these attractions close earlier at other times of the year. You should try to purchase concert tickets well in advance of your trip.

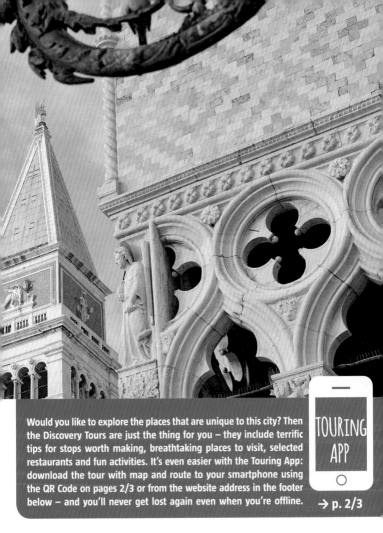

Would you like to explore the places that are unique to this city? Then the Discovery Tours are just the thing for you – they include terrific tips for stops worth making, breathtaking places to visit, selected restaurants and fun activities. It's even easier with the Touring App: download the tour with map and route to your smartphone using the QR Code on pages 2/3 or from the website address in the footer below – and you'll never get lost again even when you're offline.

TOURING APP

→ p. 2/3

Get to know Venice at its best in just one eventful day with this tour packed full of the city's highlights.

08:00am At the ❶ **Santa Lucia train station, take a Line 1** *vaporetto* **to San Silvestro**. In the morning light, the glistening façades of the palaces along the Canal Grande breeze past – there really is no better way to begin a day exploring the grandeur of this city on the lagoon! Stop for a cappuccino and a croissant at ❷ **Caffè del Doge** → p. 65, **then head northwards and go around two or three**

❶ Santa Lucia train station

❷ Caffè del Doge

❸ Pescheria

❹ Campo Santa Margherita

❺ Frari Church

❻ Scuola Grande di San Rocco

❼ Alaska

❽ Galleria d'Arte Moderna

❾ Do Mori

❿ Piazza San Marco

⑪ American Bar

⑫ Mercerie

corners to get to the ❸ **Pescheria** → p. 31. Stroll past the fishmongers' stalls *(Tue–Sat)* and enjoy this amazing feast for the eyes even if you don't plan on buying anything!

09:30am Continue walking from the market through the alleys to the ❹ **Campo Santa Margherita** → p. 52, **which is just a ten minutes' walk away. Go past Campo San Polo and the Frari Church** and then sit down at one of the tables at **Caffè Rosso** → p. 78 **on the western side**. It's a great place to observe the goings-on of daily life in Venice away from the tourist crowds.

10:30am After a short break, **make your way back to the** ❺ **Frari Church** → p. 49. It's worth it just to see Titian's pyramid-shaped tomb and the picture of Christ's Ascension above the mail altar! **Right next door** is the ❻ **Scuola Grande di San Rocco** → p. 51. Make sure to take a good look at its main hall adorned with 56 paintings by Jacopo Tintoretto.

12:30pm Afterwards, walk through the **alleyways of San Polo** with its souvenir and craftsmen's shops. **Take a little detour to Santa Croce** and check out Carlo Pistacchi's Gelateria ❼ **Alaska** → p. 64. Your next destination is one of the most impressive **palaces on the Canal Grande**, which now houses the ❽ **Galleria d'Arte Moderna** → p. 30. The collection in Ca' Pesaro contains a representative selection of 19th and 20th century art.

02:30pm A number of quaint, old wine taverns **around the Rialto bridge** have survived the various waves of modernisation intact. The oldest of these so-called *bacari* is the picture-perfect ❾ **Do Mori** → p. 63. Enjoy fabulous wine and delicious *cicchetti* at the bar!

03:30pm The *vaporetto* line 1 (Rialto Mercato station) will take you straight to the ❿ **Piazza San Marco** → p. 40. Visit **St. Mark's Basilica**, enjoy the fabulous views from the **Campanile**. Then watch the masses on St. Mark's Square from the ⑪ **American Bar** → p. 62, a standing bar **at the foot of the clock tower**.

05:00pm Fancy a bit of shopping? **Then stroll through the** ⑫ **Mercerie** → p. 70 **towards the Rialto bridge**. Almost all major fashion designers have boutiques along

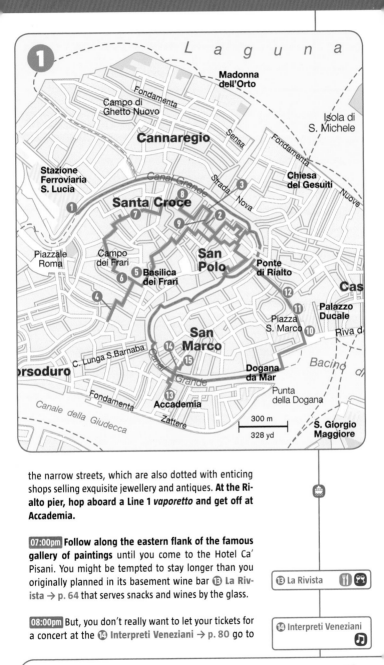

the narrow streets, which are also dotted with enticing shops selling exquisite jewellery and antiques. **At the Rialto pier, hop aboard a Line 1 *vaporetto* and get off at Accademia.**

07:00pm **Follow along the eastern flank of the famous gallery of paintings** until you come to the Hotel Ca' Pisani. You might be tempted to stay longer than you originally planned in its basement wine bar ⑬ **La Rivista → p. 64** that serves snacks and wines by the glass.

08:00pm But, you don't really want to let your tickets for a concert at the ⑭ **Interpreti Veneziani → p. 80** go to

⑬ La Rivista

⑭ Interpreti Veneziani

waste. Experience Baroque chamber music at its finest surrounded by the suggestive ambiance of a former church! Afterwards, **cross the Ponte dell'Accademia to get to San Vidal in less than five minutes**.

 Art Blu Caffè

10:00pm Time for some food now? **Close by**, the ⑮ **Art Blu Caffè → p. 77**, serves large and small snacks and good drinks. Along with fabulous views of the Campo Santo Stefano by night!

2 VENICE AHOY – AROUND THE OLD CITY CENTRE BY BOAT

START: ❶ Santa Lucia train station **END:** ❶ Santa Lucia train station	1 day Travelling time (without stops) 2 hours

Distance:
approx. 25 km/15.5 mi

COSTS: approx. 70 euros/person (day ticket, food, admission fees)
WHAT TO PACK: water bottle, rain gear or sun protection as needed

IMPORTANT TIP: Lines 4.1 and 4.2 run every 20 minutes during the day.

The best way to explore the historic heart of the city of canals is on the water. Instead of embarking on the classic route along the main artery, the Canal Grande, try a tour around the city for a change. Aboard a Line 4.1 or 4.2 *vaporetto*, you will become acquainted with the lesser-known Cannaregio district and the harbour area as well as Murano and the cemetery island as you enjoy panoramic views of Venice's most beautiful waterside promenades.

❶ Santa Lucia train station

The **starting point** for this tour is the ❶ **Santa Lucia train station**. **At the bottom of the steps, board one of the floating buses so characteristic of the city of canals called a *vaporetto*, serving Line 4.2** (Line 4.1 travels the same route, but in the opposite direction). At first, the boat chugs briefly along the Canal Grande. But immediately after passing the impressive church of San Geremia – it turns left onto the Canale di Cannaregio. Leaving the Palazzo Labia behind, the route continues into the unusually spacious and bright district – at least according Venetian standards – of Cannaregio. **You should interrupt your journey at the first stop (Ponte delle Guglie) and walk to the former Jewish ❷ Ghetto**

❷ Ghetto

A master of glass blowing at work on Murano

→ p. 47, which has a fabulous museum. Thirsty? Pop into the Jewish restaurant ❸ **Ghimel Garden** → p. 69 – it's worth it just for the garden.

Back on the *vaporetto*, pass under the triple arches of the Ponte dei Tre Archi and out into the open water. The views reach as far as the islands of Burano and Torcello, and to the airport. The boat speeds up and heads east. **Stay on as far as Fondamente Nove,** then stretch your legs on land for a few minutes. How about a look at the Jesuit church of ❹ **Chiesa (or Santa Maria Assunta) dei Gesuiti** → p. 46? Hardcore Baroque – impressive! ❺ **Titian's house** is somewhat less so.

Now head back onto the boat to glide on to ❻ **San Michele** → p. 57. By no means should you miss out on a walk across this cemetery island with its quite special atmosphere and famous graves, such as those of Igor Stravinsky and Sergei Diaghilev! **The northernmost point along this round-trip route** is the island of ❼ **Murano** → p. 58, famous for its traditional glass blowing industry. Art lovers should definitely take a look inside the

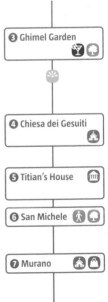

❸ Ghimel Garden

❹ Chiesa dei Gesuiti

❺ Titian's House

❻ San Michele

❼ Murano

churches of **San Pietro Martire** and **Santi Maria e Donato**. Souvenir shoppers, on the other hand, should make their way to one of the glassblowers' workshops open to visitors.

Return to the Fondamente Nove stop and take the *vaporetto* along the northern shore of the Castello district. It passes the Franciscan church called San Francesco della Vigna and navigates around the San Pietro di Castello and Isola di Sant'Elena peninsulas. Once it reaches the San Marco basin, it steers past the Biennale exhibition grounds to the west. As you pass by ⑧ **Riva degli Schiavoni**, the quay that is a popular place to go for a stroll because it is so broad, you can enjoy INSIDER TIP the parade of some of the most famous hotels in the city.

Is your stomach grumbling? Then **get off the boat one last time at San Zaccaria. Just 200 m/656 ft away via Calle degli Albanesi awaits** ⑨ **Aciugheta** → p. 62 with its tasty snacks. **Once you are back on the boat**, you will drift past the island of Giudecca before coming to the **ferry harbour and crossing under the controversial Ponte della Costituzione → p. 30 to return to** ① **Santa Lucia train station**.

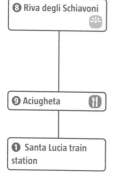

⑧ Riva degli Schiavoni

⑨ Aciugheta

① Santa Lucia train station

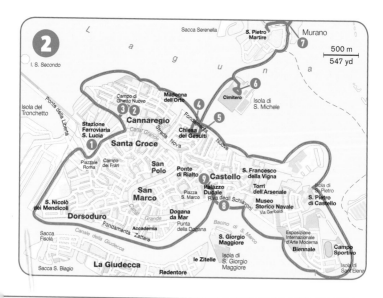

IN THE FOOTSTEPS OF PALLADIO

3

START: ❶ San Marco-San Zaccaria stop END: ❼ Skyline Rooftop Bar	3–4 hours Walking time (without stops) approx. 45 minutes
Distance: 🚢 3 km/1.9 mi on foot	

COSTS: approx. 80 euros/person (day ticket for local transportation, food, coffee, drinks, admission fees incl. monastery tour)
WHAT TO PACK: rain gear or sun protection as needed

This walking tour leads you to the magnificent sacral buildings designed by master architect Andrea Palladio from Padua. You will also get to know the two islands to the south of the old city centre, San Giorgio Maggiore and Giudecca.

Take a Line 2 *vaporetto* from the ❶ San Marco-San Zaccaria stop to cross over to San Giorgio Maggiore in a matter of minutes. As you do so, you can take in the most popular photo motif in this city on the lagoon, namely the monastery of ❷ San Giorgio Maggiore. It was built at the end of the 16th century for the Benedictines by Andrea Palladio on the picturesque island across from the Doge's Palace. **Once you have reached the church** itself, take a moment to fully appreciate the geometrical austerity of its dazzling white marble façade reminiscent of an ancient temple before you take a look at the equally impressive interior of this three-nave church with its large Tintoretto paintings.

The panoramic view from the top of the INSIDERTIP **Campanile di San Giorgio Maggiore** *(daily 9.30am–12.30pm and 2.30pm–6pm, in winter only until 4.30pm)* is just as breathtaking as the view from the Campanile of San Marco across the way.

From San Giorgio, cross to the island of Giudecca – just travel one station further on the same line. The stop at Zitelle is called this because Palladio built a convent for unmarried girls *(zitelle)* here. Its church: ❸ **Santa Maria della Presentazione**. **Stroll around the church:** INSIDERTIP Four wonderful gardens brought back to life by Francesca Bortolotto Possati, the owner of the

❶ San Marco-San Zaccaria stop

❷ San Giorgio Maggiore

❸ Santa Maria della Presentazione

wonderful Palladio Hotel & Spa, which can today be found inside the convent's walls.

4 Il Redentore

Then stroll along the beach as far as Palladio's masterpiece in Venice, the church **4 Il Redentore** *(Mon 10.30am–4pm, Tue–Sat 10.30am–4.30pm)* with the Classicist dome and brilliant marble façade. It was built in the late 16th century as a plea to God to end the plague, which was devastating at that time. Every year, on the third Sunday in July, it is the site of the Redentore Feast, which commemorates the end of the epidemic.

5 La Palanca

Then continue along the shore to the trattoria **5 La Palanca** *(Mon–Sat 12 noon–2.30pm, bar 7am–8.30pm | tel. 04 15 28 77 19 | Budget)* and enjoy the excellent lunch or snacks and, from the waterside tables, wonderful views of the Zattere. **Go through the Calle del Forno, then head left on Campo Junghans and follow along Rio del Ponte Lungo until you reach the open water. About 700 m/2300 ft further west,** you should definitely take a look at the **6 showroom** *(Mon–Fri 10am–1pm and 2pm–6pm | Fondamenta San Biagio 805)* of Fortuny, the legendary creator of luxury textiles – they are a feast for the eyes!

6 Showroom

The perfect way to end the day, **right nearby on the other side of the small canal,** is INSIDER TIP to go up to the roof of the Molino Stucky Hilton Hotel. Enjoy a pleasant

Andrea Palladio's masterpiece: San Giorgio Maggiore on the monastery island

drink in the **⑦ Skyline Rooftop Bar** *(daily, in winter Tue–Sun 5pm–1am)* as you admire the magical view of the city and its lagoon.

⑦ Skyline Rooftop Bar

---

④ EXPLORING THE LESSER-KNOWN ISLANDS IN THE LAGOON

START: **❶ Fondamente Nove stop** END: **❻ Lazzaretto Nuovo**	1/2 day Time on board 1 hour, walking time approx. 2 hours
Distance: 🡒 approx. 10 km/6.2 mi	

COSTS: approx. 50 euros/person (day ticket local transportation, food), 7 euros for a tour inside **❻ Lazzaretto Nuovo** (optional).
WHAT TO PACK: sturdier shoes for cross-country walks, rain gear or sun protection as needed
IMPORTANT TIPS: tours of **❻ Lazzaretto Nuovo** only offered Sat/Sun

---

The three islands of Murano, Burano and Torcello are well-known destinations for excursions, but the many smaller islands in the north of the lagoon are also worth a trip. They will show you the more rural side of Venice where you can walk through the trees and learn about local nature.

① Fondamente Nove stop

② Le Vignole

③ Trattoria alle Vignole

④ Sant'Erasmo

⑤ Torre Massimiliana

The best place to begin your tour is Venice's "vegetable island". It takes just 15 minutes by boat to get from the **① Fondamente Nove stop** to the island of **② Le Vignole. Walk along the main path from the jetty to the little bridge and cross over the main canal. Follow the right-hand path** through the vegetable fields to **③ Trattoria alle Vignole** *(closed Mon and Oct–Mar | tel. 04 15 28 97 07 | Budget)*. It's a good bet that the fish and meat dishes served on the simple wooden tables outside will taste particularly good alongside the view of Venice's silhouette! Only private boats with special authorization are permitted to access the famous maritime fortress of Sant'Andrea on the southern tip of the island. Constructed by the famous master builder Michele Sanmicheli in the 16th century, its canons once kept the enemies of the La Serenissima from approaching the city by sea.

The island of **④ Sant'Erasmo** → p. 59 further to the north is a very peaceful place. It is the second, but much larger garden before the doors of Venice. **Take a Line 13** *vaporetto* **from Le Vignole to get to the island's stop Capannone. Walk about 15 minutes to the south** to the **⑤ Torre Mas-**

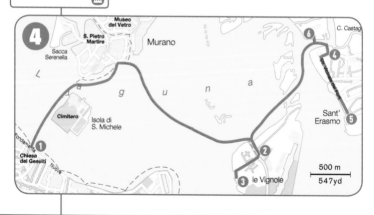

The patchwork quilt of idyllic green islands in the north of the lagoon

similiana *(April–Oct Wed–Fri 2pm–7pm, Sat/Sun 11am–7pm)*, a fortified brick tower that now hosts interesting contemporary art exhibitions.

The little island of ⑥ Lazzaretto Nuovo lies across from the aforementioned Stazione Capannone. Thanks to its strategic location, it has been used by the Venetians and different occupiers as a military base at different points in history. From the 15th to the 18th centuries, it also protected La Serenissima against epidemics as it served as a quarantine station for people and goods. For some years now, archaeologists and ecologists have been devoting more attention to this long neglected and almost forgotten island.

⑥ Lazzaretto Nuovo

As part of an "island revival" campaign, a team of local volunteers now offers highly recommendable INSIDER TIP nature and history walks from April to October at the weekend *(Sat/Sun 9.45am and 4.30pm | tel. 04 12 44 40 11 | www.lazzarettonuovo.com)*. If you wish to take part in one of these tours, then **you need to board a *vaporetto* in Sant'Erasmo heading for Lazzaretto Nuovo around 4.15pm.** During the tour, you will learn more about Venice during the plague and you will get to see some of the defensive walls and huge warehouses – in particular the so-called Teson Grande filled with museum objects – as well as a documentary film. On the half-hour nature walk along the island's outer walls, informative display boards describe the flora and fauna found in the lagoon area.

TRAVEL WITH KIDS

In Venice you will look in vain for the classical "highlights for kids in cities" such as a museum or theatre just for them, or a zoo and special tours. But Venice's completely different lifestyle will more than compensate for that.

As a rule, climbing one of the towers and admiring the view from the top (followed by icecream?) is a hit. And, they can have a lot of fun playing football or hide-and-seek with the local kids in one of the many playgrounds such as those on the *campi San Polo, Santa Margherita* and *San Giacomo dell'Orio.* Pack the best-seller "The Thief Lord" by Cornelia Funke. The exciting chase through the mysterious lagoon city will have you wanting to explore it yourself. And how about geocaching *(www.geocaching.com)?* Venice offers a number of nicely hidden destinations. Counting the bridges and fountains is an entertaining pastime.

LAGOON ADVENTURE ● ◎
(131 D–E 2–5) *(₥ 0)*

In addition to the small islands that can be reached by *vaporetto* (see chapter "Discovery Tours") many other treasures in the areas of natural and art history are waiting to be discovered in the lagoon: archaeological sights, historical fortresses, saltworks, bird reserves and traditional fishermen's huts that are still in use today. *The Operatori Naturalisti Limosa (tel. 0 41 93 20 03 | www.limosa.it, www.slowvenice.it)* and *Sestante di Venezia (tel. 04 12 41 39 87 | www.sestantedivenezia.it)* organise INSIDER TIP tours that will also fascinate children. A very special way to really get a feel for the charm of the more distant canals and islets is on board a *bragozzo*, which is the name of an old-fashioned wooden freight barge. A number of excellent organisers are listed at *www.guidetovenice.it* (heading: The Lagoon); for more information in English: *32 89 48 56 71*

LIDO ● (131 D–E4) *(₥ 0)*

A (half)day on the Lido swimming and building sand castles makes a welcome change. There is a playground next to the Planetarium on *Lungomare D'Annunzio.* Another contrast programme could be a bike outing to the south-west of the Lido, which is surprisingly green in some parts. There are two places *(noleggio cicli)* where you can hire bicycles, tandems and rickshaws for four at the Lido *vaporetto*

Off to the Lido! Canals, the lagoon and the beach island: a change of pace for kids tired of culture and museums

stop: *Gardin (Piazza Santa Maria Elisabetta 2 | tel. 04 12 76 00 05 | www.bici clettegardin.com)* and *Renato Scarpi (Viale Santa Maria Elisabetta 21b | tel. 04 15 26 80 19 | www.lidoonbike.it)*.

PALAZZO DUCALE SPECIALE
(127 D3) (*Ⓜ K8*)

Walk along "secret routes" *(itinerari segreti)* through the Doge's Palace: an adventure for youngsters (from the age of 6), even if they don't understand a word. The tours are held every morning – twice in Italian, French and English – and take you along narrow corridors to the most distant corners of the palace including the false ceiling of the Great Council Hall, and to the dark dungeon where Giacomo Casanova once spent some time. Bookings at the information counter at the entrance to the palace or from abroad by *tel. 0 41 42 73 08 92* as well as online under *www.palazzoducale.visitmuve.it*

ROWING, ALLA VENEZIANA

Two time-honoured rowing clubs give short courses lasting only a few days to teach beginners and children (from around ten) how to manoeuvre a *sandolo*, *mascareta* or *gondola* elegantly over the water. *Società Canottieri Bucintoro* (126 A6) (*Ⓜ H10*) *(Zattere 261 | tel. 04 15 20 56 30 | www.bucintoro.org | one person 3–5 hours, 100 euros; group lesson 85 euros/person)* and *Canottieri F. Querini* (123 E5) (*Ⓜ M5*) *(Fondamente Nove 6576e | tel. 04 15 22 20 39 | www.canot tieriquerini.it | 8 lessons, 1.5 hours each, 130 euros; 1 lesson, 1.5 hours 80 euros)*.

THROUGH THE CANALS BY BOAT
(121 D4) (*Ⓜ F3*)

Exploring the labyrinth of canals in a rented boat is an adventure. The best address for renting rowing boats or motorised vessels is *Giampetro Brussa (Calle Fondamenta Labia 331 | tel. 0 41 715 87 | www.brus saisboat.it)* next to Ponte delle Guglie.

FESTIVALS
& EVENTS

JANUARY

Capodanno in Spiaggia (New Year at the Beach): All visitors on the Lido are given snacks and warm drinks from 11pm

6 Jan: At the *Festa della Befana* on Sant'Erasmo, children are given presents by the good witch *(befana)*, and a fire is lit.

CARNIVAL

The legendary ⭐ *Carnival* with hundreds of events, balls and an ocean of masks all over the city starts with the INSIDER TIP *Volo dell'Angelo*, the "Flight of the Angel", at which a young woman dressed in historic costume floats above St. Mark's Square. All dates day by day: *www.carnevale.venezia.it*

MARCH/APRIL

On the last Sunday in March or the first Sunday in April: *Su e Zo per i Ponti* – running race "up and down the bridges". *www.suezo.it*

Maundy Thursday: *Benedizione del Fuoco* – when St Mark's Basilica glows in the light of thousands of candles.

INSIDER TIP *Yachting in Venice:* Boat exhibition on a weekend in the middle of April. With yachts to look at and board, and a programme for children.

25 April: *Festa di San Marco* with a solemn mass in the Basilica, gondola races on the Canal Grande and festivities on the Piazza

MAY/JUNE

1 May: ● *Sagra dea Sparesea* – "Asparagus Festival" in Cavallino with an open race and regatta, celebrations and fireworks

On a Sunday in May or June: *Vogalonga* – the great open regatta from San Marco across the lagoon (see p. 44)

Sunday after Ascension: *Festa della Sensa* – "Marriage with the Sea" with a historical fleet sailing from San Marco to the Lido

MID-MAY – EARLY NOVEMBER

⭐ *Art biennale* in uneven years in the former shipyard Arsenale in the east of the district of Castello, and spread all over the city. Exhibitions, private views and events, all based on contemporary art: painting, sculptures, installations, dance and theatre. The exhibition pavilions are also architecturally interesting. *www.labiennale.org*

Not only Carnival: Venice's calendar of festivities has something for everyone – from the exuberant to the more contemplative

JULY

Second Sunday: ● *Fishermen's Festival at Malamocco* with regatta and fish feast
Third Sunday: *Redentore* "Feast of the Saviour" with beautiful procession to the Redentore church; amazing display of INSIDER TIP *fireworks* on the night before

SEPTEMBER

First weekend: *Regata Storica* – thousands of festively decorated boats with historically-costumed crews glide down the Canal Grande
Eleven days of the *International Film Festival* on the Lido. www.labiennale.org/it/cinema
Third Sunday: *Fish Festival* with vast quantities of *pesce fritto*, deep-fried fish

OCTOBER

First or second Sunday: ● *Wine Festival* on Sant'Erasmo with music, dancing, feasting and a regatta
Late October: *Venice Marathon* starting in Stra. www.venicemarathon.it

NOVEMBER

21 Nov: *Madonna della Salute* – procession over pontoons to the church followed by a feast with raisin donuts and wine

PUBLIC HOLIDAYS

1 Jan	*Capodanno*
6 Jan	*Epifania*
March/April	*Pasquetta* (Easter Monday)
25 April	*Liberazione* (Day of liberation from fascism)
1 May	*Festa del Lavoro*
2 June	*Giorno della Repubblica* (Day of the Republic)
15 Aug	*Ferragosto*
1 Nov	*Ognissanti*
8 Dec	*Immacolata Concezione* (Immaculate Conception)
25 Dec	*Natale*
26 Dec	*Santo Stefano*

LINKS, BLOGS, APPS & MORE

LINKS & BLOGS

www.fotocommunity.com/photos/venice Fabulous photos, sometime bright and cheerful, sometimes melancholy. These artistic photos reveal the city in all her many different moods – and new ones are constantly being added

www.veneziaunica.it/en The official tourist and travel information of Venice gives a good overview

www.cosmotourist.com/ excursion tips, restaurant reviews, hotel evaluations, personal travel experiences. Here you browse through almost 200 impressions

www.timeout.com/venice Up-to-date, hand-picked descriptions of major attractions, hotels, restaurants, bars and shops

www.veniceonline.it An excellent resource for everything you want to know about being a tourist in Venice. It has the entire city's transport information as well as maps, photos, videos, audio guides, cultural events, restaurants, webcams and much more

short.travel/ven21 In the so-called Thorntree-Forum of the Lonely Planet community you'll find more than 13 000 different postings on Venice: from concrete hotel tips and train connections up to recommendations for a romantic honeymoon alla venezia

short.travel/ven2 Those who wish to explore the less well-known places in Venice and the lagoon will find a whole range of thematic city plans here, as well as a directory of addresses for a more sustainable, alternative form of tourism

www.europeforvisitors.com/venice Private travel-planning site for Venice with lots of useful advice, including information for cruise ship tourists and sections like "The top 11 Mistakes"

venicewiki.org Even if you don't speak Italian, this Wiki will provide you with

Regardless of whether you are still preparing your trip or already in Venice: these addresses will provide you with more information, videos and networks to make your holiday even more enjoyable.

much valuable and useful information ranging from Venetian songs to a dialect dictionary

www.venetiancat.blogspot.com is the popular blog by author and newspaper contributor Cat Bauer who has lived on the Canal Grande in Venice for a number of years. The blog has been featured in a number of international publications and is an insider's view of the expat life in Venice

www.ogvenice.com/blog Tasteful private travel guide with blog and detailed texts about topics like Murano glass, bookstores or Venetian aperitifs

VIDEOS & MUSIC

short.travel/ven3 The official video of the Flight of the Angel that opens the Carnival. Very close to the event, and the footage quality is excellent

short.travel/ven4 An amateur cameraman shows how grotesque the vast cruise liners look in the lagoon

short.travel/ven5 Video of the first trial run of the MOSE flood protection project. The mammoth undertaking is to protect Venice from floods

short.travel/ven23 In five minutes, 13 beautiful spots on and around Venice's canals are captured – in slow motion and accompanied by the "Chorus of the Hebrew Slaves" from Verdi's Nabucco

APPS

Venice Giracittà is an English-language audio guide has more than four hours of information on the city: from busy squares to narrow lanes to mysterious places

The Essential Green Travel Guide ♻ Eco-conscious Venice travellers in particular will love this iPhone App: It shows everything a hip LOHAS person needs – from weekly markets selling organic produce, slow food restaurants and fair trade products to yoga studios

mTrip Guide The ultimate Venice App for iPhone and Android not only has the typical travel guide information on offer, but also many tools like a travel journal and the possibility to send your snapshots as e-postcards

TRAVEL TIPS

ARRIVAL

✈ A number of different major airlines such as British Airways (www.britishairways.com) offer regular flights from the UK to Venice, from around £50 upwards, with prices averaging out at around £150 per person. Alitalia (www.alitalia.com) and several other international European airlines offer regular but not direct flights. Several no-frills airlines however do fly directly, e.g. easyJet (www.easyjet.com) and Ryanair (www.ryanair.com), although not necessarily to Venice's main international airport. Some major carriers in the USA and Canada also offer direct flights as well as flights to major centres (Rome, London) and connecting flights to Venice.

Venice's international Marco Polo Airport is on the northern border of the lagoon in Tessera (http://airport-venice.com). Many cheaper flights are to Treviso airport located 20 km/12.4 mi inland (www.trevisoairport.it).

From here there is also a bus (8 euros, 15 euros return | www.atvo.it) to the Piazzale Roma. As well as the very expensive water taxis, the vaporetti of the Alilaguna line (www.alilaguna.it) operate from Marco Polo airport to the islands of Murano (8 euros) and Lido (15 euros), and in Venice itself to St. Mark's Square (15 euros). You can purchase tickets online at www.venice link.com, and slightly cheaper than in Venice.

🚗 Venice is reached by car over the Ponte della Libertà causeway. We recommend that day visitors park in one of the – quite expensive and often full – multi-storey car parks near the old town around the Piazzale Roma or on Tronchetto Island. Both have recently been connected by a "people mover", an almost 900 m/2950 ft long cable car on stilts (ticket: 1.50 euros). The car parks on the mainland in Fusina, Treporti and Punta Sabbioni are less expensive. A modern tram line connects Mestre and Venice via the Ponte della Libertà.

🚆 Venice can easily be reached by train from major cities all over Europe. But if you really want something different, try the Venice Simplon Orient Express (www.belmond.com). It is a privately-run train of historic and beautifully-restored 1920s, 30s & 50s coaches, providing a classic luxury train experience between London, Paris, Innsbruck and Venice. It links London and Venice roughly once a week between March

RESPONSIBLE TRAVEL

It doesn't take a lot to be environmentally friendly whilst travelling. Don't just think about your carbon footprint whilst flying to and from your holiday destination but also about how you can protect nature and culture abroad. As a tourist it is especially important to respect nature, look out for local products, cycle instead of driving, save water and much more. If you would like to find out more about eco-tourism please visit: www.eco tourism.org

and November, the complete journey taking 24 hours and costing around 2500 euros per person one way.

BANKS & MONEY

There are a great number of cash dispensers throughout the city and major credit cards are accepted almost everywhere.

CALENDAR OF EVENTS

The best way to find out about events, etc. is through the daily newspapers *Il Gazzettino* and *La Nuova Venezia* and the (Italian/English) pamphlets *Venezia News*, *Un Ospite di Venezia*, *Venezia da Vivere* and Meeting *Venice*. The last two are available free of charge at all arrival points, in many hotel receptions, at travel offices, etc.

CITY PASS VENEZIA UNICA

This personalized card is the cheapest way to take advantage of the public services in Venice. It is valid for seven days, making it easy for you to pick and choose your own agenda. Deals start with a basic offer, the San Marco City Pass for 27.90 euros. It includes free admission to the Doge's Palace, three other museums on St. Mark's Square, three churches, the Museo Querini Stampalia and one ticket to the casino. Various more expensive options include more museums, use of the vaporetti, airport transfers and the city's WiFi network. You can also add parking tickets and guided tours. The pass can be purchased online *(www.veneziaunica.it)*

BUDGETING

Vaporetto	6.60 £/8.40 $ *for a single ticket*
Gondola	70 £/90 $ *for a 30-minute trip*
Snack	from 2.60 £/3.40 $ *for a panino at the bar*
Entrance	2.60 £/3.40 $ *for entrance to one of the major churches*
Wine	from 1.60 £/2 $ *for a small glass of white wine at the bar*
Espresso	0.90 –1.75 £/1.10–2.25 $ *for a cup at the bar*

or at the vaporetti stops Tronchetto, Piazzale Roma, Rialto, Lido, Burano and Punta Sabbioni.

CUSTOMS

EU citizens can import and export goods for their personal use tax free (e.g. 800 cigarettes, 10 L of spirits over 22%). Visitors from other countries must observe the following limits, except for items for personal use. Duty free are: max 50 ml perfume, 200 cigarettes, 50 cigars, 250 g tabacco, 1 L spirits (over 22% vol) and 2 L of any wine.

EMBASSIES & CONSULATES

BRITISH HONORARY CONSUL
Piazzale Donatori di Sangue 2/5 | 30171 Venice-Mestre | tel. (39) 041 505 5990 | www.gov.uk/world/italy

U.S. CONSULAR AGENCY

at Venice Marco Polo Airport | General Aviation Terminal | Viale Galileo Galilei 30 – 30173 Tessera (VE) | tel. (39) 041 541 5944 | https://it.usembassy.gov/embassy-consulates/milan/consular-agency-venice/

EMERGENCY SERVICES

Emergency: *tel. 112* | Police: *tel. 113* | fire brigade: *tel. 115* | ambulance *tel. 118*

GONDOLAS

For many people, a romantic ● ride in a gondola is one of the highlights of a visit to Venice. A half-hour ride in a gondola in a group of four to six people will usually cost around 80–100 euros. Individuals can obtain a seat in a gondola with other passengers by booking online, e.g. at *www.localvenicetours.com* (28 euros/person).

The gondolieri wait for their passengers at the Piazzetta San Marco, in front of the Hotel Danieli, behind St Mark's Square in the Bacino Orseolo, as well as along the Canal Grande at the Piazzale Roma, near the railway station at Campo Santa Sofia, by Rialto Bridge and the San Tomà, Giglio and Vallaresso *vaporetto* stops.

There are gondola ferries, so-called *traghetti*, that carry passengers across the Canal Grande for 2 euros per crossing at San Marcuola, near Santa Sofia next to the Ca' d'Oro, at the Riva del Carbon next to Rialto Bridge, near San Tomà, between San Samuele and Ca' Rezzonico, as well as by Santa Maria del Giglio.

GUIDED TOURS

You can book officially authorised, Eng-lish-speaking guides from the *Cooperativa Guide Turistiche (tel. 04 15 20 90 38 | ww.guidevenezia.it)*. The price for a personal tour lasting two hours is 141 euros.

HEALTH

The EHIC, the EU insurance card issued by the British authorities, is valid in Italy. It is recommended that you take out travel healthcare insurance to cover the costs of private treatment. The consulate will help you find an English-speaking doctor. In emergencies, the Santi Giovanni e Paolo Hospital can be reached under *tel. 04 15 29 41 11*, the health centre on the Lido under *tel. 04 12 38 56 68*. The *pronto soccorso* section is responsible for emergency admission. Information on chemist's open outside of the regular hours is posted or available from the telephone information service at *tel. 192*.

HIGH WATER

Acqua alta is almost part of everyday Venetian life in the winter. If there is the threat of flooding, warning sirens are sounded throughout the entire city. The nightmare usually lasts for a few hours. There are maps in some *vaporetto* stops showing where there are wooden bridges that make it possible to reach your destination without getting your feet wet – even when the city is under water. The water-level forecast can be found on the internet under *www.ilmeteo.it/portale/marea-venezia*

INFORMATION IN ADVANCE

www.turismovenezia.it is the official website of the tourism association, *www.comune.venezia.it* the digital visiting card of the city administration with many useful links. The official tourist website of the city with detailed instructions on how to purchase the city pass (see p. 109) as well as information about local attractions and events is *www.veneziaunica.it*. Information on public transportation routes, timetables and tariffs is available under *www.actv.it*; there is a detailed description of the eleven city museums at *www.visitmuve.it*. Information, in Italian and English, on art, sporting and other events, can also be found at *www.meetingvenice.it*. *www.veniceonline.it* provides a helpful overview with many links ranging from hotel bookings to the weather forecast and programme of events.

INFORMATION IN VENICE

The central contact address by phone is the *Tourist Contact Center (daily 9am–2pm | tel. 04 15 29 87 11)*. Local information centres are operated by the VELA company. The main ones are at the station *(daily from 7am–9pm)*, in

the centre at the Museum Correr *(daily from 9am–7pm)*, at the Piazzale Roma *(daily from 7.30am–7.30pm)* and at Marco Polo airport *(daily from 8.30am–7pm)*. Ticket desks and machines for vaporetti and buses are also to be found all over the city and on the islands. You will find a map with the precise locations at *tripplanner. veneziaunica.it*. Tourist information, ticket reservations and purchases for all sorts of events are also possible at *www. veneziaunica.it* or in English or Italian at *tel. 0 41 24 24*.

Central information office of the Tourism association (not open to the public): *Azienda di Promozione Turistica APT (Palazzetto Carmagnani | Fondamenta Cornér-Zaguri 2637 | 30 124 Venezia | www.turismovenezia.it)*

Complaints about unsatisfactory public services or improper treatment of tourists can be submitted via e-mail to *com plaint.apt@turismovenezia.it*. During its normal business hours, the tourism association APT also offers assistance under *tel. 04 15 29 87 26*.

FIT IN THE CITY

Why not learn to do what the gondolieri do? Two traditional rowing clubs, *Società Canottieri Bucintoro (tel. 04 15 20 56 30 | www.bucintoro.org)* and *Associazione Canottieri Giudecca (tel. 04 15 28 74 09 | www.canottierigiudecca.com)* give short courses where even beginners can learn how to steer a *sandolo*, a *mascareta* or *gondola* elegantly over the water and through the canals. A few hours of cycling along the seashore can be wonderful alternative to the many, many hours spent wandering through

the city. Bicycles can be rented at the Lido *vaporetto* stop: *Gardin (tel. 04 12 76 00 05 | www.biciclettegardin.com)* on Piazza Santa Maria Elisabetta 2 and *Renato Scarpi (tel. 04 15 2 62 80 19 | www.lidoonbike.it)* at Viale Santa Maria Elisabetta 21b. From there, you can pedal off towards the south as far as the picturesque villages Malamocco and Alberoni, and if you have the time and are fit enough, ride past the Lido di Pellestrina along the stone causeways *(murazzi)* to the small fishing town of Chioggia.

INTERNET ACCESS & WIFI

It possible for you to log in to the WiFi network and access the internet near St Mark's Square, free of charge. The only condition is that you purchase a museum ticket or pass online under *www.veneziaunica.it*. Most hotels now offer either a computer with internet for guest use or provide WiFi access (password protected) for smartphones, tablets or laptops.

PHONES & MOBILE PHONES

Phone boxes are also becoming a rarity in Venice. The few that remain operate by a phone card *(carta telefonica)*, which you can buy for 5 or 10 euros from post offices, kiosks and in bars.

To phone the UK from Venice, use the country code 0044, for calls to the US 001. The country code for Italy is 0039, followed by the participant's full number including the '0' of the area code.

PORTERS

These helpers are sometimes extremely useful in this city of bridges and narrow streets. They can be found at the railway station, Piazzale Roma, by the Accademia, near San Marco and the Hotel Danieli. The price for transporting each piece of luggage within the old town is 24 euros.

POSTAGE

Stamps *(francobolli)* can be bought in post offices or tobacconist's shops. Postage for postcards and standard letters to EU countries is 1 euro.

WEATHER IN VENICE

	Jan	Feb	March	April	May	June	July	Aug	Sept	Oct	Nov	Dec
Daytime temperatures in °C/°F	6/43	8/46	12/54	17/63	21/70	25/77	28/82	28/82	24/75	18/64	12/54	7/45
Nighttime temperatures in °C/°F	1/34	2/36	5/41	10/50	14/57	17/63	20/68	19/66	17/63	12/54	7/45	3/37
Sunshine hours/day	3	4	4	6	7	9	10	9	7	5	3	2
Precipitation days/month	6	6	7	8	9	7	6	5	6	8	9	7
Water temperature in °C/°F	9/48	8/4	10/50	13/55	17/63	21/70	23/73	24/75	21/70	18/64	14/57	11/52

PUBLIC TRANSPORT

By far the most practical form of transportation, and at the same time the one with the most flair, are the scheduled boats (vaporetti), or water buses, operated by the municipal transport companies ACTV *(www.actv.it)*, although they are often overfull. They operate around two dozes lines on the Canal Grande and the main secondary canals, and also connect the old town to the Lido, the lagoon islands and the mainland. However, a single ride costs an impressive 7.50 euros. So it's cheaper to buy a commutation ticket: a 24-hour ticket will cost 20 euros, a two- or three-day ticket 30 or 40 euros, a week's ticket 60 euros. Depending on the line, regular service starts in the morning between 5 and 7am, and ends between 8pm and 1am at night. Important for night owls: boats on the Canal Grande, the Giudecca Canal and to the Lido and northern lagoon islands also run all through the night on the *linee notturni*.

TAXIS

The water taxis, so-called *motoscafi*, are a rather expensive proposition and are most suitable for small groups (up to a maximum of 10 people). Additional charges are made for more than 2 passengers, trips at night, telephone bookings, large pieces of luggage, etc. The most important stops are at the Piazzale Roma, the railway station, near Rialto Bridge, in San Marco, at the Lido and the airport. *Tel. 04 15 22 23 03, 6pm–9am and Sat/Sun 04 12 40 67 12 | www.motoscafivenezia.it*

TIPPING

A service charge is normally included, but waiters, hotel maids, gondolieri etc. are naturally pleased if you reward them for friendly service. Five to ten percent is usual in restaurants.

WEATHER, WHEN TO GO

Venice has a moderate, Mediterranean climate. The hot sirocco wind blowing from Africa and the high humidity level can make it rather sticky in summer; the humidity is still there in winter when Venice can be cold and damp and, sometimes, foggy. From the climatic point of view, the best times to visit La Serenissima are April/May and September/October but some weeks in winter, when the air is crystal clear, have a very special charm. The weather on the web: *www.tempoitalia.it*

CURRENCY CONVERTER

£	€	€	£
1	1.15	1	0.88
3	3.45	3	2.64
5	5.75	5	4.40
13	14.95	13	11.44
40	46	40	35.20
75	86.25	75	66
120	138	120	105.60
250	287.50	250	220
500	575	500	440

$	€	€	$
1	0.90	1	1.10
3	2.70	3	3.30
5	4.50	5	5.50
13	11.70	13	14.30
40	36	40	44
75	67.50	75	82.50
120	108	120	132
250	225	250	275
500	450	500	550

For current exchange rates see www.xe.com

USEFUL PHRASES ITALIAN

PRONUNCIATION

c, cc	before e or i like ch in "church", e.g. ciabatta, otherwise like k
ch, cch	like k, e.g. pacchi, che
g, gg	before e or i like j in "just", e.g. gente, otherwise like g in "get"
gl	like "lli" in "million", e.g. figlio
gn	as in "cognac", e.g. bagno
sc	before e or i like sh, e.g. uscita
sch	like sk in "skill", e.g. Ischia
z	at the beginning of a word like dz in "adze", otherwise like ts

An accent on an Italian word shows that the stress is on the last syllable.
In other cases we have shown which syllable is stressed by placing a dot
below the relevant vowel.

IN BRIEF

Yes/No/Maybe	Sì/No/Forse
Please/Thank you	Per favore/Grazie
Excuse me, please!	Scusa!/Mi scusi
May I ...?/Pardon?	Posso ...? / Come dice?/Prego?
Good morning!/Good afternoon!/ Good evening!/Good night!	Buon giorno!/Buon giorno!/ Buona sera!/Buona notte!
Hello! / Goodbye!/See you	Ciao!/Salve! / Arrivederci!/Ciao!
My name is ...	Mi chiamo ...
What's your name?	Come si chiama?/Come ti chiami
I would like to .../Have you got ...?	Vorrei .../Avete ...?
How much is ...?	Quanto costa ...?
I (don't) like that	(Non) mi piace
good/bad	buono/cattivo
broken/doesn't work	guasto/non funziona
too much/much/little/all/nothing	troppo/molto/poco/ tutto/niente
Help!/Attention!/Caution!	aiuto!/attenzione!/prudenza!
ambulance/police/fire brigade	ambulanza/polizia/vigili del fuoco
Prohibition/forbidden	divieto/vietato
danger/dangerous	pericolo/pericoloso

DATE & TIME

Monday/Tuesday/Wednesday	lunedì/martedì/mercoledì
Thursday/Friday/Saturday	giovedì/venerdì/sabato

Parli italiano?

'Do you speak Italian?' This guide will help you to say the basic words and phrases in Italian.

Sunday/holiday/ working day	domęnica/(giọrno) fęstivo (giọrno) feriạle
today/tomorrow/yesterday	oggi/domạni/ięri
hour/minute	ọra/minụto
week/month/year	settimạna/mẹse/ạnno
What time is it?	Che ọra è? Che ọre sọno?
It's three o'clock/It's half past three	Sọno le tre/Sọno le tre e mẹzza
a quarter to four/ a quarter past four	le quạttro mẹno un quạrto/ un quạrto ạlle quạttro

TRAVEL

open/closed	apęrto/chiụso
entrance/exit	entrạta/uscịta
departure/arrival	partẹnza/arrịvo
toilets/ladies/gentlemen	bạgno/signore/signọri
(no) drinking water	ạcqua (non) potạbile
Where is ...?/Where are ...?	Dov'è ...?/Dọve sọno ...?
left/right/straight ahead/back	sinịstra/dẹstra/drịtto/indiętro
close/far	vicịno/lontạno
bus/tram	bus/tram
taxi	tạxi/tassì
bus stop/taxi stand	fermạta/postęggio tạxi
parking lot/parking garage	parchęggio/parchęggio copęrto
street map/map	piạnta/mạppa
train station/harbour/airport	stazịone/pọrto/aeropọrto
schedule/ticket/supplement	orạrio/bigliętto/supplemento
single/return	sọlo andạta/andạta e ritọrno
train/track/platform	trẹno/binạrio/banchịna
I would like to rent ...	Vorrẹi noleggiạre ...
a car/a bicycle/boat	ụna mạcchina/ụna biciclętta/ụna bạrca
petrol/gas station	distributọre/stazịone di servịzio
petrol/gas / diesel	benzịna/dięsel/gasọlio
breakdown/repair shop	guạsto/officịna

FOOD & DRINK

Could you please book a table for tonight for four?	Vorrẹi prenotạre per stasẹra un tavọlo per quạttro?
on the terrace/by the window	sụlla terrạzza/ vicịno ạlla finęstra
The menu, please	Il menù, per favọre
bottle/carafe/glass	bottịglia/carạffa/bicchięre

knife/fork/spoon	coltello/forchetta/cucchiaio
salt/pepper/sugar	sale/pepe/ zucchero
vinegar/oil/milk/cream/lemon	aceto/olio/latte/panna/limone
cold/too salty/not cooked	freddo/troppo salato/non cotto
with/without ice/sparkling	con/senza ghiaccio/gas
vegetarian/allergy	vegetariano/vegetariana/allergia
May I have the bill, please?	Vorrei pagare/Il conto, per favore
bill/tip	conto/mancia

SHOPPING

Where can I find...?	Dove posso trovare ...?
I'd like .../I'm looking for ...	Vorrei .../Cerco ...
Do you put photos onto CD?	Vorrei masterizzare delle foto su CD?
pharmacy	farmacia
baker/market	forno/ mercato
shopping centre/department store	centro commerciale/grandemagazzino
grocery	negozio alimentare
supermarket	supermercato
photographic items/newspaper shop	articoli per foto/giornalaio
100 grammes/1 kilo	un etto/un chilo
expensive/cheap/price	caro/economico/prezzo
organically grown	di agricoltura biologica

ACCOMMODATION

Do you have any ... left?	Avete ancora ...
single room/double room	una (camera) singola/doppia
breakfast/half board/ full board	prima colazione/mezza pensione/
(American plan)	pensione completa
at the front/seafront/lakefront	con vista/con vista sul mare/lago
shower/sit-down bath/balcony/terrace	doccia/bagno/balcone/terrazza
key/room card	chiave/scheda magnetica
luggage/suitcase/bag	bagaglio/valigia/borsa

BANKS, MONEY & CREDIT CARDS

bank/ATM/pin code	banca/bancomat/ codice segreto
cash/credit card	in contanti/carta di credito
bill/coin/change	banconota/moneta/il resto

HEALTH

doctor/dentist/paediatrician	medico/dentista/pediatra
hospital/emergency clinic	ospedale/pronto soccorso
fever/pain	febbre/dolori

diarrhoea/nausea/sunburn	diarrea/nausea/scottatura solare
inflamed/injured	infiammato/ferito
plaster/bandage/ointment/cream	cerotto/fasciatura/pomata/crema
pain reliever/tablet/suppository	antidolorifico/compressa/supposta

TELECOMMUNICATIONS & MEDIA

stamp/letter/postcard	francobollo/lettera/cartolina
I need a landline phone card	Mi serve una scheda telefonica per la rete fissa
I'm looking for a prepaid card for my mobile	Cerco una scheda prepagata per il mio cellulare
Where can I find internet access?	Dove trovo un accesso internet?
dial/connection/engaged	comporre/linea/occupato
socket/adapter/charger	presa/riduttore/caricabatterie
computer/battery/rechargeable battery	computer/batteria/accumulatore
at sign	chiocciola
internet address (URL)/e-mail address	indirizzo internet/indirizzo email
internet connection/wifi	collegamento internet/wi-fi
e-mail/file/print	email/file/stampare

LEISURE, SPORTS & BEACH

beach/bathing beach	spiaggia/bagno/stabilimento balneare
sunshade/lounger/cable car/chair lift	ombrellone/sdraio/funivia/seggiovia
(rescue) hut/avalanche	rifugio/valanga

NUMBERS

0	zero	17	diciassette
1	uno	18	diciotto
2	due	19	diciannove
3	tre	20	venti
4	quattro	21	ventuno
5	cinque	30	trenta
6	sei	40	quaranta
7	sette	50	cinquanta
8	otto	60	sessanta
9	nove	70	settanta
10	dieci	80	ottanta
11	undici	90	novanta
12	dodici	100	cento
13	tredici	1000	mille
14	quattordici	2000	duemila
15	quindici	½	un mezzo
16	sedici	¼	un quarto

STREET ATLAS

The green line indicates the Discovery Tour "Venice at a glance"
The blue line indicates the other Discovery Tours
All tours are also marked on the pull-out map

Exploring Venice

The map on the back cover shows how
the area has been sub-divided

D E F

100 m
109 yd

Cimitero

Cimitero

15

2

2

2

2

Isola di San Michele

3

Canale delle Fondamenta Nuove

Pal. Donà

R. Dona

Pal. Donà

12 13 N Fondamente Nove

Calle larga dei

Casa Tiziani

Calle Bres

Calle Cose

Calle Colombina

Ramo de Crosera

Cristo

C.te Cristo

Volto

Botteri

Stella

Fondamente Nuove

4

San Lazzaro dei Mendicanti

Furlan

Ramo de Crosera

Mendicanti

Fondamenta

Mendicanti

Ospedale

5

C.llo Widmann

Widmann

Calle

Calle

Corte Cortese

Corte Nuova

Calle Pindemonte

S. Gabriella

Pal. Grifalconi

Ospedale Civile

2

Nuove

Santa Maria del Pianto

Santa Giustina

d. Piovan C. larga

G. Gallina

Scuola Grande di San Marco

Bartolomeo Colleoni

Santi Giovanni e Paolo (San Zanipolo)

Calle Capucine

Capucine

B. 22

Soranzo-Axel

C. d. Squero Vecchio

C.po San Zanipolo

Saliz. S. Zanipolo

S. M. della Visitazione (Ospedaletto)

Calle Nicolo

Calle Moschete

Mazza

d. Forno

Campo

Sanudo

Pal. Pisani

C.te Erbe

Corte Borella

Calle d. Cavallo

C.te Cappello

C.te Vinanti

Bres

C. Testori

R. d. Moschete

C. d. Forno

C. S. Giustina

avanti

Santa Giustina

di

6

Pal. Marcello-Pindemonte

Marcello

Borgo

Rio

di

F. Felzi

C. Carampo

Pal. S. Moros

Barbaria

C. d. Cafetier

Campo

S. Giustin.

Francesco

123 127

Ex Con

S.

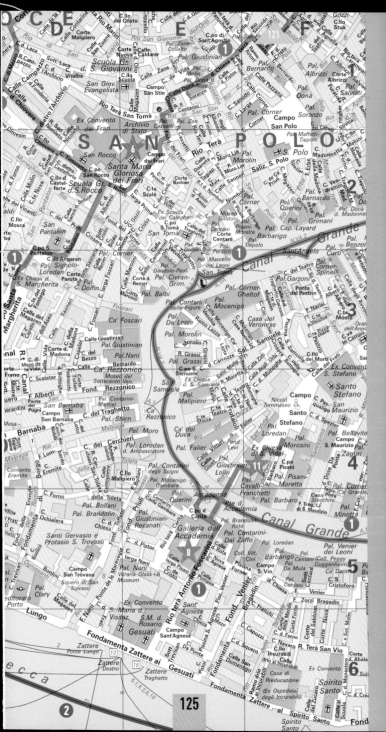

A

Ex Convento
Campo San Francesco
d. Vigna
Fond. Case Nuove
Celestia

S. Francesco della Vigna

Pal. Gritti Pal. della Nunziatura
Corte della Confraternita

Corte Da Ponte

Calle

R. 2
Sagredo
Oratorio
Cimitero

Pal. Contarini

S. Giustina

e Nova

Convento

Giovanni dei lieri di Malta

S. Giorgio dei Furlani

Sant' Antonino

Pal. Gritti

Campo Bandiera e Moro
S. Giov. in Bragora

Pal. Gabrielli

Pal. Magno

Pal. Erizzo
San Martino

C. Arsenale

Ingresso di Terra
F. di Fronte

C A S T E L (continuing) **T E L**

Arsenale

Darsena

Grande

Canale delle Galeazze

Darsena Vecchio

Arsenale Vecchio

Torri dell'Arsenale

Campo de Fronte l'Arsenal

Ca' di Dio

Ex Forni Militari

Tana

Campo della Tana

Museo Storico Navale

Palazzetto dello Sport

C.po S. Biagio

San Biagio

Fondamenta

Corte Nuova

Calle S. Francesco di Paola

S. Francesco di Paola

C.llo d. Pace

2

Riva Ca' di Dio

Riva S. Biagio

Via

Riva

dei

Sette

Martiri

C.llo Squero

La Marinaressa

Donna Partigiana

Villino canonica

Giuseppe

Garibaldi

Viale Giuseppe Garibaldi

Largo Decorati al Valor Civile

Giardini

Arsenale

Canale di San Marco

100 m
109 yd

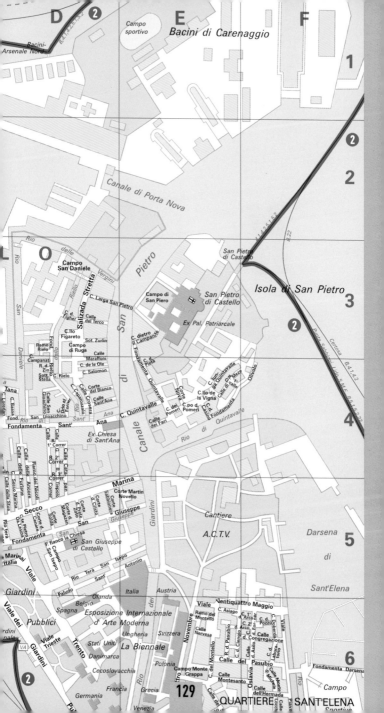

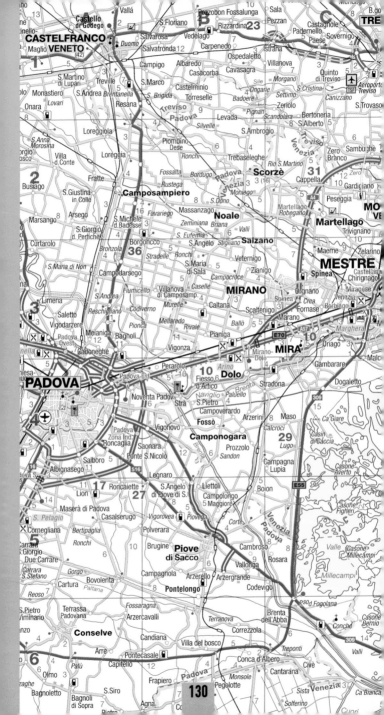

This index lists a selection of the streets and squares shown in the street atlas.

Italiano / Deutsch		English / Français
Strada a quattro corsie / Vierspurige Straße		Road with four lanes / Route à quatre voies
Strada diattraversamento / Durchgangsstraße		Thoroughfare / Route de transit
Strada principale / Hauptstraße		Main road / Route principale
Altre strade / Sonstige Straßen		Other roads / Autres routes
Parcheggio / Parkplatz	P	Parking place / Parking
Informazioni / Information	i	Information / Information
Ferrovia principale con stazione / Hauptbahn mit Bahnhof		Main railway with station / Chemin de fer principal avec gare
Altra ferrovia / Sonstige Bahn		Other railway / Autre ligne
Traghetto per automobili / Autofähre		Car ferry / Bac pour automobiles
Traghetto per persone (Vaporetto) / Personenfähre (Vaporetto)		Passenger ferry (Vaporetto) / Bac pour piétons (Vaporetto)
Pontile per le gondole - Stazione terminale / Gondelanlegestelle - Endhaltestelle		Landing stage for gondolas - Terminus / Embarcadère pour les gondoles - Terminus
Chiesa interessante - Altre chiesa / Sehenswerte Kirche - Sonstige Kirche		Church of interest - Other church / Église remarquable - Autre église
Sinagoga / Synagoge		Synagogue / Synagogue
Posto di polizia - Ufficio postale / Polizeistation - Postamt		Police station - Post office / Poste de police - Bureau de poste
Ostello della gioventù - Ospedale / Jugendherberge - Krankenhaus		Youth hostel - Hospital / Auberge de jeunesse - Hôpital
Monumento - Faro / Denkmal - Leuchtturm		Monument - Lighthouse / Monument - Phare
Caseggiato, edificio pubblico / Bebaute Fläche, öffentliches Gebäude		Built-up area, public building / Zone bâtie, bâtiment public
Zona industriale / Industriegelände		Industrial area / Zone industrielle
Parco, bosco / Park, Wald		Park, forest / Parc, bois
Cimitero / Friedhof	+ + + + +	Cemetery / Cimetière
Cimitero ebraico / Jüdischer Friedhof	L L L L L L	Jewish cemetery / Cimetière juif
MARCO POLO Giro awentura 1 / MARCO POLO Erlebnistour 1		MARCO POLO Discovery Tour 1 / MARCO POLO Tour d'aventure 1
MARCO POLO Giro awentura / MARCO POLO Erlebnistouren		MARCO POLO Discovery Tours / MARCO POLO Tours d'aventure
MARCO POLO Highlight	☆	MARCO POLO Highlight

FOR YOUR NEXT TRIP...

MARCO POLO TRAVEL GUIDES

The travel guides with
Insider
Tips

INDEX

This index lists all sights, museums and places featured in this guide. Numbers in bold indicate a main entry.

WRITE TO US

e-mail: info@marcopologuides.co.uk
Did you have a great holiday?
Is there something on your mind?
Whatever it is, let us know!
Whether you want to praise, alert us to errors or give us a personal tip – MARCO POLO would be pleased to hear from you.
We do everything we can to provide the very latest information for your trip.

Nevertheless, despite all of our authors' thorough research, errors can creep in. MARCO POLO does not accept any liability for this. Please contact us by e-mail or post.
MARCO POLO Travel Publishing Ltd
Pinewood, Chineham Business Park
Crockford Lane, Chineham
Basingstoke, Hampshire RG24 8AL
United Kingdom

PICTURE CREDITS
Cover photograph: Canal Grande and Santa Maria della Salute Church (Schapowalow: M. Rellini)
Photos: DuMont Bildarchiv: S. Lubenow (76/77); GALLERIA D'ARTE L'OCCHIO (18 top); Getty Images: S. Blanco (99), Maremagnum (90/91), T. Moore (3), M. Secchi (64); K. Hausen (1 below); huber-images: G. Baviera (43, 81), M. Carassale (62, 74), F. Cogoli (58/59, 106 below), L. Da Ros (9, 53), O. Fantuz (68 l.), Fischer (20/21), Gräfenhain (12/13, 42, 106 top), J. Huber (5, 34), Kremer (40, 104), M. Rellini (26/27, 37, 102/103), S. Scata (103), R. Schmid (23, 107), G. Simeone (flap left); © iStockphoto: Lynn Seeden (18 centre); Laif: P. Adenis (49), Degiorgis (18 below), G. Gerster (105), N. Hilger (46), Kirchgessner (8), H. Kloever (70/71), Zinn (55); Laif/Contrasto: Savino (25); Laif/Le Figaro Magazine: Martin (33 © VG Bild-Kunst, Bonn 2017, 67, 84); Laif/Palladium: Burg + Schuh (31); laif/Polaris: M. Silvestri (flap right); Laif/SZ Photo: J. Giribas (82/83); Laif/Zurita: dePablo (4 top, 17); Look: J. Greune (11), K. Jäger (10, 95, 118/119), K. Johaentges (14/15, 100/101), K. Wothe (51); Look/age fotostock (2); mauritius images: J. Warburton-Lee (4 below, 60/61); mauritius images/age (7, 56); mauritius images/Alamy: HelloWorld Images Premium (19 top); mauritius images/Caia Image: T. Adeline (19 below); mauritius images/Cubolmages (72, 89); mauritius images/Cultura: A. Weinbrecht (102); mauritius images/imagebroker: S. Lubenow (68 r.); mauritius images/robertharding: C. Morucchio (104/105); Schapowalow: M. Rellini (1 top); Schapowalow/4Corners: L. Linder (6); Schapowalow/SIME: M. Carassale (25), L. Da Ros (38/39)

3rd edition, fully revised and updated 2018
Worldwide Distribution: Marco Polo Travel Publishing Ltd., Pinewood; Chineham Business Park, Crockford Lane, Basingstoke, Hampshire RG24 8AL, UK. Email: sales@marcopolouk.com
© MAIRDUMONT GmbH & Co. KG, Ostfildern
Chief editor: Marion Zorn
Author: Walter M. Weiss; editors: Kirstin Hausen, Nikolai Michaelis
Programme supervision: Stephan Dürr, Lucas Forst-Gill, Susanne Heimburger, Nikolai Michaelis, Martin Silbermann, Kristin Wittemann; picture editor: Gabriele Forst, Anja Schlatterer; What's hot: wunder media, München
Cartography street atlas and pull-out map: © MAIRDUMONT, Ostfildern
Cover design, p. 1, pull-out map cover: Karl Anders – Büro für Visual Stories, Hamburg; design indside: milchhof:atelier, Berlin; design p. 2/3, Discovery Tours: Susan Chaaban Dipl.-Des. (FH)
Translated from German by Robert McInnes, Jennifer Walcoff Neuheiser and Mo Croasdale
Editorial office: SAW Communications, Redaktionsbüro Dr. Sabine A. Werner, Mainz: Julia Gilcher, Cosima Talhouni, Dr. Sabine A. Werner; prepress: SAW Communications, Mainz, in cooperation with alles mit Medien, Mainz
Phrase book in cooperation with Ernst Klett Sprachen GmbH, Stuttgart,
Editorial by Pons Wörterbücher

MIX
Paper from responsible sources
FSC® C124385

DOS & DON'TS ✋

These things are best avoided in Venice

DON'T TAKE YOUR SHIRT OFF WHEN WALKING AROUND THE OLD TOWN

No matter how hot its, bare male or over-exposed female torsos or beachwear are taboo on the streets of the *centro storico*. And going into a church in that kind of getup is not an option; you won't be let in.

DON'T ORDER PASTA AS A MAIN COURSE

It might be all right to fill up on a plate of pasta in a cheaper restaurant or tourist trap and then simply pay and go. In better-class restaurants, however, there is an unwritten law forbidding this. Here, as everywhere else in Italy, pasta is a *primo piatto* and is followed by a main course of meat or fish. If you need a snack, a *panino* or a couple of *tramezzini* at the bar are a better idea.

DON'T GET TAKEN IN BY FALSE TRAFFIC WARDENS

So-called *abusivi*, illegal traffic wardens, get up to no good around the car parks on Tronchetto Island. Sometimes dressed in orange jackets, sometimes in white shirts, white-and-blue caps and armbands, they look almost like the real thing and attempt to manoeuvre unsuspecting newcomers to the taxi boats of a private shuttle service. This will make the trip to San Marco or to the islands much, much more expensive than by *vaporetto*.

DON'T EAT ON THE PIAZZA

An ever-increasing number of tourists have started taking a break on and near St Mark's Square and this has caused the authorities to ban sitting, drinking and eating on the Piazza, its steps, in the arcades, or on the Piazzetta by the jetties. The Giardini ex Reali, 150 m/492 ft away, has officially been declared the place where you can tuck in to your food.

DON'T DRAG YOUR WHEELIE BAG OVER THE BRIDGES

Please carry it over the many little bridges in Venice. Dragging it over the steps will indeed cause the bridges to crumble – imagine how many millions of wheelie bag wheels bang against the steps every year. To say nothing of the noise they make.

DON'T DODGE FARES

You might well be tempted, but be careful! Inspections are sometimes made on board *vaporetti* and, if you get caught without a ticket, it costs at least 50 euros.

DON'T FEED THE PIGEONS

It was a photographic ritual for generations of tourists: feeding pigeons with specially-bought bird food. But now the authorities have finally had enough of the flocks of birds and all the dirt. Those who get caught feeding the pigeons will be fined 500 euros. And street salesmen are not allowed to sell food for our feathered friends either.